PRAISE FOR PAUL FERRINI'S BOOKS

"Paul Ferrini's writing will inspire you to greater insights
and understandings, to more clarity and a greater resolve to make
changes in your life that can truly change the world."
NEALE DONALD WALSCH

"These words embody tolerance, universality, love and
compassion—hallmarks of all Great Teachings. Paul Ferrini is a
modern-day Kahlil Gibran—poet, mystic, visionary, teller of truth."
LARRY DOSSEY, M.D.

"Paul Ferrini leads us skillfully and courageously beyond shame,
blame and attachment to our wounds into the depths
of self-forgiveness. His work is a must-read for all people who
are ready to take responsibility for their own healing."
JOHN BRADSHAW

"The most important books I have read. I study them like a bible!"
ELISABETH KÜBLER-ROSS, M.D.

"Paul Ferrini reconnects us to the Spirit Within, to that place where
even our deepest wounds can be healed."
JOAN BORYSENKO, PH.D.

"I feel that this work comes from a continuous friendship with the
deepest part of the Self. I trust its wisdom."
COLEMAN BARKS.

"Paul Ferrini's wonderful books show a way to walk lightly
with joy on planet earth."
GERALD JAMPOLSKY, M.D.

Book Design by Paul Ferrini
and Lisa Carta

Library of Congress Control Number
2007922755

ISBN # 978-1-879159-68-6

Heartways Press
9 Phillips Street, Greenfield MA 01301
www.heartwayspress.com

Manufactured in the United States of America

REAL HAPPINESS

A Roadmap for Healing Our Pain

& Awakening the Joy That Is Our Birthright

PAUL FERRINI

Table of Contents

To the Reader

This book is written for you if you have an earnest desire to bring greater joy and happiness into your life. It may also help someone else that you know, a friend or a loved one.

Real Happiness is geared not only to my generation—the baby boomer generation—but to my children's generation. Like me, you may have a son or a daughter in their late teens or twenties who is struggling to heal and find greater happiness in life. Or perhaps you are a young adult with a parent who is struggling. For adults of all ages, 18–81, this book offers a simple but profound roadmap for the journey of healing and empowerment. It offers straight talk on all the important issues, such as dealing with fear, shame, anger, guilt and the root causes of addiction. It also offers concrete practices that you can do to awaken joy and peace in your heart and mind.

To find happiness, you must believe that happiness is possible and you must be willing to examine the causes of your unhappiness. There are no other prerequisites.

A Definition of Happiness

This book is not about the kind of happiness you see on billboards or television commercials. It has nothing to do with the overly romanticized or idealized type of happiness. It has to do with being present right now for the ups and downs of life in a loving and compassionate way. It is about being ourselves fully and being responsible for what we are creating in our lives.

I like to call it *Real Happiness* because it is about being real as a human being and coming face to face with our fear and our pain. It is about being willing to heal our wounds so that we can reconnect with the joy that is our birthright.

Of course, being real isn't easy. To be real we need to feel safe enough to cry our tears as well as to sing our songs of gratitude and praise. We need to be strong enough to stop blaming others and brave enough to learn our lessons.

Real happiness means overcoming our negativity and beginning to count our blessings so we can experience the mysterious beauty of life. It means learning to surrender, to let go of the need to control, and to allow our lives to unfold in their own natural, organic way. It is about becoming fully, uniquely and exquisitely human!

What is Real?

The best definition of "real" comes from one of my favorite children's books *The Velveteen Rabbit** by Margery Williams. When the Rabbit asked what it meant to be real, the Skin Horse replied:

> "Real isn't how you are made.... It's a thing that happens to you. When a child loves you for a long, long time, not just to play with, but REALLY loves you, then you become Real."
> "Does it hurt?" asked the Rabbit.

---

* From *The Velveteen Rabbit* by Margery Williams. Doubleday & Company, Inc. Garden City, New York. Reissue edition (January 6, 1958). Used by permission.

"Sometimes," said the Skin Horse, for he was always truthful. "When you are Real you don't mind being hurt."

"Does it happen all at once, like being wound up," he asked, "or bit by bit?"

"It doesn't happen all at once," said the Skin Horse. It takes a long time. That's why it doesn't happen often to people who break easily, or have sharp edges, or who have to be carefully kept. Generally, by the time you are Real, most of your hair has been loved off, and your eyes drop out and you get loose in the joints and very shabby. But these things don't matter at all, because once you are Real you can't be ugly, except to people who don't understand.

Real Happiness is hard to come by, but it is long lasting. As the Skin Horse tells us, "Once you are Real you can't become unreal again. It lasts for always."

PART 1

Happiness
is a Journey

Happinees is a journey.
The mountaintop is just one place
on the journey. The valley is another.
There are many ups and downs on the journey.
Better get used to it.

No Hoops

You don't have to jump through any hoops to be happy. You don't need to pay money to be happy. You don't have to believe in some old religion or even some new one.

If you believe in God or in Jesus, or Buddha, or Moses or Mohammed, it will help you on your journey to happiness. But belief in God or religion is not a prerequisite.

What do you need to believe in?

That's simple. *You need to believe in you.* You need to accept yourself just the way you are.

No More Stories

When I say, "accept yourself," I am talking about radical self-acceptance.

That means that you have to be willing to drop your story of who you think you are and let go of all the reasons why you believe that you can't be happy.

Radical self-acceptance means getting to know and value yourself on a deeper level.

I am asking you to do something simple and bold: let go of the "old you" so that the "new you" can be born.

The old you is a bunch of stories you and other people made

up about yourself. None of these stories is true. These stories just keep your unhappiness in place. So give them up.

Come to this book naked, empty. Come just as you are. Let the wrapping paper and the window dressing come off.

You will not need them here.

Showing Up

To be happy you need to be willing to show up for your life. You cannot run away from yourself or from others. You can't crawl into a cave and disappear. You can't think that other people control your happiness. They don't.

There is only one person who controls your happiness or lack of it and that is you.

To be happy, you need to show up for life and take responsibility for what you think, feel, say and do.

You can't blame anyone else for your woes.

Blame and shame keep you locked into unhappiness. They are a big part of the story that needs to go.

Here are four things you need to learn to do to be happy and you might as well start right now.

1) Show up for your life. (Stop running away.)

2) Take responsibility for your life. (Stop blaming others.)

3) Stop thinking others can make you happy. (They can't.)

4) Accept yourself as you are right now. (It's the place where you start on the journey.)

Stop Beating Yourself Up

I am sure there are things that have happened in your life that you aren't too proud of. I am sure that you feel guilty about these events in your life and you probably beat yourself up for the mistakes that you have made. That is what most people do.

Well, that must stop. It is time to accept your mistakes and learn from them. If you learn from your errors, you won't keep making them over and over again.

Instead of feeling bad about something that you said or did, make the commitment right now not to say or do that again. Make the commitment right now to understand the fears you have that trigger the behavior that hurts others or yourself. Make the commitment to befriend those fears and learn to hold them with understanding and compassion so that you do not hurt yourself or lash out at others.

When fear comes up, learn to see it and sit with it. Don't try to make it go away or try to give it to someone else. Your fear belongs to you. It is your responsibility.

Being Afraid Is Not Bad

It's not bad to be afraid. Everyone has fear come up on a daily basis. So stop running away from your fear or beating yourself up for having it.

Fear is part of life. It is part of consciousness. You are going to need to learn to live with fear.

If you push your fear away or try to give it to others, you will strengthen it. You might think that you are shoving it into a place where it will never be seen or heard from again.

But you are wrong.

The more you shove, the more energy you give to it. And it is only a matter of time when it erupts like a volcano.

So do yourself a favor. Save yourself an emotional breakdown. Be with your fear as it comes up. Learn to dance with it. Learn to get your arms around it. Your fear will not hurt you once you have made friends with it.

It is possible to experience your fear without giving away your responsibility or your power. You can walk with your fear and it is by walking with it that you move through it.

Fears come and go. Be present with them and learn from them and they will not undermine your life.

Happiness Is a Journey

We all think of happiness as a state of mind and heart and indeed it is. A peaceful mind and a joyful heart are major components of happiness.

But happiness is more than that. It is a journey. It is a process.

And that means that you are beginning in a certain place and you are going to end in a different place. No matter how happy or unhappy you are, that is simply where you start the journey.

So please accept where you are starting on the journey and do not compare yourself to anyone else. Each person starts in a unique place. And for him or her that is the best and only place to start.

Do not ask "Why can't I start the journey more happy?" That's like asking yourself to hit home runs when you are just learning to swing the bat.

Be patient. You have some very important skills to learn. And you will learn them if you are willing.

Anyone can learn to hit the ball. It's just a matter of time and practice.

Patience

Because this is a journey, you are going to have to be patient. You are not going to get there yesterday. Stop putting that kind of pressure on yourself.

Take the journey one step at a time. Along the way, there will be wonderful vistas, times when your mind is peaceful and your heart is joyful. But there will also be times when the view leaves a lot to be desired, times when you feel sad and confused.

Those are the times that will require your vigilance and your commitment, because those are the times when you want to give up. Those are the times when you might lose hope.

I am telling you this because I don't want you to have unrealistic expectations. This is a journey that goes up and down. It does not go straight to the mountaintop.

The mountaintop is just one place on the journey. The valley is another. There are many ups and downs, many mountains and valleys, on the journey. Better get used to it.

You will have highs and you will have lows. But you will learn to hold both the highs and lows with compassion. That way, the highs will not puff your ego up and the lows will not devastate you.

As you get used to the journey, you will become a better traveler. And so you will be able to move faster and more skillfully.

We don't start you at the plate with a 95-mile per hour (MPH) fastball. We throw you a 20 or 30 MPH ball until you get your timing and learn to hit it. When you do, we speed the pitch up to 40 or 50 MPH. In the end you will learn to hit that 95 MPH fastball. But that is the end of the journey, not the beginning.

And while it's good to have a vision of the future and to see where you are going, you have to make your peace with where you are. You have to learn to take the first few baby steps along the path.

What Does Not Work

There are many self-help books that tell you that you can be happy now and yes, of course, that is true. But if you were happy now, you would not need to be reading those books or this one.

Many people give you affirmations to repeat, as if affirmations could overcome your unhappiness or beat it into submission. This simply doesn't work. Indeed, it often leads to even greater frustration.

The truth of the matter is that the longer we resist our unhappiness, the more unhappy we are going to get. So let's stop resisting it.

Step one on the journey is simply to admit that you are unhappy and/or that you are not as happy as you would like to be.

Here's what I don't want you to do: I don't want you to *pretend to be happy* when you are not. I don't want you to put on a *happiness mask* because it won't help. It may trick some of the people in your life, but it's only a temporary disguise, and it is bound to fail. They will eventually find out what's really going on with you. So why waste time and try to cover up the truth.

Admit the truth to yourself and to others. That is the best way to start the journey—with honesty. Start by being real and authentic.

The Next Step

Once you have accepted your unhappiness, the next step is to inquire into it and find out where it comes from. There are many reasons for our unhappiness. Here are a few:

- Guilt over the Past/Unforgiveness of Self
- Resentment/Unforgiveness toward Others
- Shame due to Physical/Emotional/Sexual Abuse
- Excessive Self-Criticism
- Excessive Criticism of Others
- Fault Finding Attitude
- Need to Blame and Shame
- Unworthiness/Lack of Self Esteem
- Leading a Stressful Life
- Infidelity/Sex Addiction
- Obsession with Money
- Workaholism
- Not Taking Responsibility/Being a Victim
- Abusing Drugs/Alcohol or other Substances
- Fearfulness/Paranoia
- Negative Thinking
- Post Traumatic Stress Disorder
- Schizophrenia, Depression or other Mental Illness

The list could go on and on. I assume there's enough there already that you will find relevant. If so, circle the ones that apply.

If not, add to the list.

Then, take a look at the words you have circled and ask "What is the cause or origin of this?"

For example, let's take the first item on the list: *Guilt over the Past/Unforgiveness of Self.* This is one of the major causes of unhappiness for many of the people I have worked with. One woman I counseled had lost her daughter over 50 years ago in an accident that was no one's fault. Yet she was still blaming herself for her daughter's death.

My friend's trauma led her to erect a wall between herself and others. Whenever anyone got close, she would run away. That wall kept her feeling "safe," but it also kept out the intimacy that she so deeply wanted.

The cause of our unhappiness is often a core wound or a traumatic event such as an experience of loss, abuse, neglect or abandonment. As we uncover our own wound/trauma, we learn to ask, "What dysfunctional behaviors does this lead to? How does this limit or control my life?"

For some people, it is important to seek a therapeutic environment to work through the shame or trauma that they have been carrying around for years.

If that means you, please be brave and ask for help. You do not have to try to heal alone. There are many others who have similar wounds and traumas. Find a loving and accepting environment where you can learn to bring forgiveness to yourself.

The Power of Forgiveness

Most of our wounds and traumas require some kind self-forgiveness, as well as the forgiveness of others, in order to be healed.

We can't be happy right now if we are always dragging around the past. We have to lay our burden down so that we can be more fully alive here and now.

Wounds are traumas that need to be acknowledged and forgiven. Both parts of the process are necessary.

If you are in denial of your wounds, you can't be happy, because you will be driven by the shame/anger/fear attached to them. On the other hand, once you know the story and feel the pain of the wound, it's time for healing and forgiveness.

Many people get off track when they try to blame others for the pain they have experienced. But blaming others delays the healing process and often makes it more difficult.

Some people are able to forgive others readily, but they are unable to forgive themselves. They hold themselves hostage to mistakes they have made in the past. This too delays and complicates the healing process.

Whatever the wound, you must come to peace with it, for no other reason than it happened. You cannot change what happened in the past. You must accept it.

When you accept and forgive, you create the possibility that you can heal and move on.

A Simple Forgiveness Exercise

Now is a good time to make a list of your unresolved forgiveness issues. So buy yourself a journal and get busy.

Write across the page:

"I am willing to forgive _____ for _____"

Then, fill in the blanks. Write down the name of the person and the nature of his/her trespass against you. Write this sentence out for every person you are ready and willing to forgive.

Now write:

"I ask forgiveness from _____ for _____"

Then, fill in the blanks. Write this sentence out for each person you have hurt and whose forgiveness you want.

These sentences are your declaration to yourself, to others and to the world that you are ready to forgive and to be forgiven for the past. Once you have written these words, you are responsible for them, so don't write them unless you can stand by them.

From now on, you are agreeing to be open to give and receive all of this forgiveness whenever the opportunities present themselves to you. You may contact some of the people or you may not. But when they come into your life, whether the event is planned or spontaneous, remember these words and abide by them.

You are not to be attached to whether or not others decide to forgive you. That is their choice. You can apologize to them and ask for their forgiveness, but the choice to forgive is theirs, and they must live with the choice that they make.

Your only leverage is with yourself. You can decide to forgive the people who have hurt you. If you need to express your anger and pain to them first, please do so.

And then tell them you are not going to carry any more resentment. Tell them you hope that they will learn from their mistakes and that you will continue to pray that they do.

Then detach. Let them go. Set them free to live the life they choose to live. You do not have to be held hostage any more by the choices they make.

If anger or resentment comes back, then there is more forgiveness necessary. The forgiveness process takes time and the issues often run very deep.

Don't expect that it will take 5 minutes to let go of the deep psychological patterns that were constructed over a period of 20 or 30 years. Just keep forgiving more deeply as each layer comes up for healing.

Many people say they have forgiven when they are still holding onto their pain, their shame, their anger or their victimhood. This does not work.

You cannot let go of the past and hold onto your grievances at the same time.

Forgiving Yourself

Forgiving others is just the beginning of this process. The hardest person to forgive is yourself. All forgiveness in the end comes down to this. You can forgive everyone who has hurt you and they can forgive you for your trespasses. But if you cannot forgive yourself, you cannot heal fully.

So now let's do the hard one. Write the following words across the page of your journal:

"I am willing to forgive myself for _____."

Make a list of everything you are ready and willing to forgive yourself for.

Working with Resistance

If you feel that a lot of resistance to forgiving comes up, please make that resistance conscious by doing the version of the exercise that follows. Write across the page these words:

"I am *not ready* to forgive _____for _____.

Be honest and make your list of everyone you still blame, resent, and are unwilling to forgive.

Now write these words:

"I am *not ready* to forgive *myself* for _____."

Make a list of everything you are not willing to forgive yourself for.

This, you might say, is your homework for the future. You will get to it eventually. But you cannot start here, because you cannot forgive anyone, including yourself, until you are ready to do so.

Forgiveness work is challenging. It rarely happens quickly or neatly. It is often a lifetime process with many ups and downs and a few untidy moments. It is not easy to forgive and often we don't want to.

But sooner or later we realize that not forgiving is like leaving a huge boulder in our heart. It makes it very hard for us to breathe. Life without forgiveness is not a happy life.

So, every once in a while — maybe once or twice per month — revisit your journal and look at all the people you have not been able to forgive and all the reasons why you can't forgive yourself and ask "Am I ready to forgive any of these people? Am I ready to forgive myself?"

One of these days, the honest answer will be "Maybe." And that's the turning point.

When you are ready and willing to forgive, it gets much easier. You start to feel some genuine movement. You begin to feel lighter and brighter. You begin to have hope that change is possible.

The boulder in your heart begins to shrink and you can finally take a deep breath. Believe me, that is a milestone on the journey.

Breathing deeply is a lot trickier than you think. And you can't be happy if you are unable to take a deep breath at least once or twice every day.

Not Making an Identity in the Wound

The choice to heal is a powerful one. But not everyone makes this choice. Often when people come to grips with their pain, they get stuck in blame and shame. They get attached to their story. They will tell you with or without tears in their eyes "I can't be happy because my uncle abused me when I was six." They believe that they are damaged goods. They establish an identity in the wound. They become their story.

The attachment to the wound is as counterproductive as denial of the wound. Both are dysfunctional and prevent healing from happening.

No, *we don't want to deny the wound,* the cause of our unhappiness, *but we don't want to be attached to it for the rest of our lives either.*

We investigate the wound so that we can understand it and heal from it. *We go through the pain, not to stay in it, but to come out the other side.* This is important.

Our journey of healing cannot progress if we do not "move through" our pain. In the end, we have to forgive and let go.

There is no other way to heal.

Living in the Present

We heal the past so that we can live fully in the present. And then the only question is "Am I happy now?"

I like to ask a parallel question: "Am I loving myself right now?"

That is because I know that when I am loving myself, it is easy for me to be happy. It is easy for me to have a positive attitude and work cooperatively with whatever life is presenting.

So my mantra becomes "Am I loving myself right now?" And when the answer is "No," the question helps me remember what I need to do.

Another equally important question is "Am I forgiving myself now?" That's a good one to ask when the wound or the grievance resurfaces.

Many people think that forgiveness is a one-time act. It would be nice if this was true, but it is hardly the case. Forgiveness is a daily, moment-to-moment process.

In one moment I can forgive you or myself and in another moment I can be harboring resentment or guilt. So I need to keep practicing forgiveness. And I need to practice forgiveness with forgiveness. I must forgive myself for not doing it perfectly. I must forgive myself for being stubborn and holding onto grievances.

We must remember that forgiveness is not just a goal that we strive for. It is a practice that we do each day of our lives. And, like in anything else, we have ups and downs.

Some days we are forgiving and some days we are not. Sometimes we can be gentle with ourselves and others, and other days we can be insensitive, even cruel.

No matter what our experience is, we must accept it.

Tomorrow, we may do better. Tomorrow, we may be able to learn from our mistakes.

But today all we can do is acknowledge our mistakes and try not to beat ourselves up for making them. Today, the best that we can do is to forgive ourselves for making a mess of things.

One Day at a Time

As people in recovery know, we must take one day at a time. We cannot make the healing process go any faster than it wants to go.

This requires a lot of patience with ourselves and others.

If we are too much in a hurry, we run the risk of skipping steps. And when we skip steps, parts of us remain unhealed.

That's okay. We will try to skip steps anyway and, consequently, we will fall down on our faces. We will have to learn the hard way that skipping steps does not work We will have to learn that being in a hurry wastes a lot of time.

All of us have tried to make the river move faster or attempted to swim against the tide, but we eventually learn that it does not work. We have to "go with the flow." Anything else just increases our frustration and exhausts our energy.

The healing process is a lot like a river. At times it meanders and even seems to loop back on itself. But at other times it moves with sound and fury, overcoming any obstacles in the way.

We have to be prepared for all possibilities. Yet we also have to show up for what is happening right now.

For those who want to heal, *now* is the most important time. For healing does not happen in the past. It happens in the present.

Now is the time for our healing. Now is the time for forgiveness.

Giving a Present to Ourselves

When we keep our attention focused on what is happening right now, we give ourselves the greatest present.

Bringing yourself into the present moment brings you all the gifts of life. Because that is where our sins are forgiven. That is where our guilt is released. That is where healing happens. That is where miracles are given and received.

Of course, to really be present here and now, you must drop your story.

When you drop your story, you are naked and undefined. You could be anyone or anything. All things are possible.

Even if you were an alcoholic or a drug addict in the last moment, in this moment you can drop that. You can drop any behavior, any mask, any way of defining who you are.

In the present, you can stop all addictions, simply by choosing not to use.

If you choose to use, you drag the past forward. When you do that, your addiction is running your life and you are condemned to live in a repetitive pattern. Is that not what an addict is?

Yes, you have a choice in each moment, but it may not feel like a choice to you. That is not surprising when you keep making the same choice over and over again.

You need to ask yourself "Who is making this choice?"

If you answer that question honestly, you will have to admit that the person who is "choosing" is that little kid inside you who feels overwhelmed and terrified by life.

That kid does not want to feel the pain. S/he doesn't want to be in the present, because that would mean meeting the pain head on.

So what does s/he do? S/he reaches for something that offers immediate gratification. Maybe it's a drink, a joint, or a pill. Maybe it's an orgasm or a piece of chocolate cake.

We seek "pleasure" because we don't want to feel our pain. That is the beginning of the repetitive cycle. That is where the addict is created.

Not Running Away from the Pain

The cause of any addiction can be traced back to the moment when the wounded child began to stuff his/her pain. For most of us that goes back a long way.

But you are not a little kid anymore, are you? You are an adult. You have choices, right? You don't have to run away. You can be present. You can face life, whatever it is dishing out. Right?

Please be honest with yourself.

If you are brutally honest, you will realize that—as much as you tried to grow up and leave that unpleasant little kid back in the past—s/he lives just under your skin. Indeed, you might have to admit that your adult mask is wearing thin. It is only a matter of time before your pain bleeds through and everybody sees it.

It's time to face the reality that this abused or abandoned little kid is running your life, undermining your career and your marriage, maybe even taking out his or her anger on your son or your daughter.

Perhaps you try to tune that kid out so that you don't have to feel the pain. You might use a pill or a drink to escape, or you might bury yourself in work 20 hours each day. We all have our unique patterns of escape/avoidance.

Is this pattern the cause of your unhappiness? Probably not. It is more a symptom of it.

The cause is the original wound. It is the hurt that made you curl up into a fetal position and decide that you were going to protect yourself from any future pain by sealing off your heart. The original pain built the wall around you.

The wall looks different for everyone. But if you want to heal, you have to take the wall down. You have to stop working or drugging yourself to death. You have to stop your pattern of avoidance, which keeps the pain frozen and locked in.

In the end, you have to feel the pain you have been running away from. You need to come face to face with the wound so that you can heal it.

Opening Pandora"s Box

Now, I know that you don't want to go there. Like most people, you are scared to look into that deep, black hole where your pain is hidden.

You have worked very hard, trying to grow up quickly and carve out an elaborate adult mask that prevents your pain from being seen by others. Indeed, when you look in the mirror, you probably think the masked figure reflected there is who you really are.

You have forgotten that it is all a sham. It is your false self, your persona, that you see in the mirror, not the wounded little kid. You would rather forget about that kid and the messy wounds that lurk in the depths of your heart.

You don't want to open Pandora's box. You know that, if you do, it will no longer be business as usual. You are understandably afraid that you will lose it and your life will come crashing down around you.

Ironically, that is exactly what will happen if you don't open the box. That is what will happen if you stay in your head and refuse to feel your pain. Something inside will simply explode.

But that hasn't happened yet, so you are likely to keep the self-deception going. It's easier to hide behind your professional mask. It's easier to pretend that everything is okay, even though in the depths of your heart you know that it isn't.

You might lie awake at night listening to the heart-rending cries of the child, but you still show up for work and give all your buddies high fives. My friends, this is called DENIAL.

When denial no longer works, you slip into depression. There are no more high fives in the morning. You show up for work, but you are like a Zombie going through the motions.

Sooner or later the shell of denial either explodes or cracks and breaks apart.

The Shattering of the False Self

The good news is that when the shell of denial cracks open *the real you* is liberated. It may not be pretty, but it is the real McCoy.

Humpty Dumpty cannot sit on the wall forever. In time, he becomes an addict, a drunk, or an adulterer. Sometimes he really goes wacko and ends up in a mental hospital.

The mask will shatter. The persona will become unglued. The volcanic tears of the child will erupt like Mt. Vesuvius.

That is the moment of our healing crisis when we are forced to face our pain finally and completely. In that moment, our old self dies and our new self rises like the phoenix from the ashes. That is the moment when we are reborn as an authentic person, in touch with our pain and the pain of others.

That is when we become fully human.

Until then, the little kid we are trying to hide inside has us on a string that runs from our private parts to the top of our head. That string moves up and down and all around and we move with it, just like a marionette.

We might as well admit it—we are hooked.

The specific form of our denial/avoidance doesn't matter. What matters is that we are stuck in it. We are on the merry-go-round, going in circles. We are too dizzy to get off and we can't stop the ride.

We have reached the moment when we either get on our knees and pray or we call out for help. Sometimes it's a good idea to do both!

Getting Help

I tell my students, "Don't be afraid to pull your mask off and reach out to someone. Tell the truth to your spouse, to your best friend, to a therapist. Tell them that you are really stressed out and that your coping mechanisms are not working any more. If you are abusing a substance, tell them you are hooked on alcohol, pot, or prescription drugs. Let the cat out of the bag before it grabs you by the throat.

"Don't wait for a full-scale emotional breakdown. Don't wait for your life to be totally shattered.

"Cut your losses. Stop the bleeding. Get off the merry-go-round before it spins out of control and your life is in danger. Don't let pride hold you back from seeking help.

"The wounds that you do not heal will be passed on to your children and your children's children. This is serious business. For their sake, if not for yours, get the help you need before it is too late.

"Every choice that you make matters, but this choice will be the most important choice of your life."

Reclaiming the Child

When you acknowledge the pain in your life and ask for help, you begin to make friends with the wounded little kid who did not get the love and attention that s/he needed growing up. You can begin to see and have compassion for all the pain, shame and fear this kid is carrying. You begin to make friends with the little girl or guy who controls the strings.

This isn't easy because we don't like to look at the war zone inside our hearts. We don't like that kid because s/he has so many negative emotions and behaves so badly.

Now, you can begin to change your relationship to that child. You can stop intellectualizing and come into your heart. You can feel the pain you have avoided.

And then you can learn to give the kid a big hug and to reassure him or her that s/he is loveable and that it is not his/her fault that everything is so scary and painful.

Instead of running away from the child, you can embrace him or her. You can make peace. You can bring adult and child back together as one.

This is an extraordinary piece of psychic integration. It takes time and it takes work, but the rewards are astounding.

Every day, you can meet the child in your heart and spend a few moments listening and speaking affectionately with him/her. After a while, you begin to see that this little child—once hostile and out of control—has become more loveable.

That is because you have taken the time to listen to him/her and bring love to the wounded parts of yourself. You have become the bringer of love. You have become the mommy or daddy you never had.

Synergy

We can see clearly now that addiction and the related patterns of avoidance of pain are not the cause of unhappiness. They are the symptoms.

The cause of unhappiness is self-betrayal. That betrayal starts with the abandonment of the inner child and continues through all forms of denial and addiction.

As you learn to love and accept yourself, the betrayal stops. The little kid gets the attention s/he needs. The division within the psyche begins to heal. A wonderful synergy occurs.

The little kid begins to feel safer and begins to play. Simultaneously, the adult becomes less morose and more joyful. This integration of child and adult is called re-parenting. In the process of re-parenting, you are becoming your own loving parent.

As you care for the child within, the little kid begins to have more trust in you. S/he isn't afraid that you will abandon her, as mommy or daddy did. So s/he invites you to take the strings back. Then, you no longer feel like a marionette, being jerked around by some force that you cannot understand or control.

You come back into your power. The divided aspects of your psyche — child and adult, conscious and unconscious, heart and mind — fuse back together into one whole. You stop being a victim. You stop making excuses for why you can't change. You stop dragging your past around with you. You drop your story. That enables you to be real and authentic. It empowers you to tell the truth to yourself and others.

You begin to step up to the plate and hit that 95 MPH fastball. You can even hit those nasty sliders and curve balls that life unexpectedly hurls at you.

You realize that you have both the right and the responsibility to be you. You can't live the way someone else wants you to live. You can't let others make decisions for you. You have to step up to the plate just the way you are and take your chances.

You know that you will have good days and bad days. You learn to be present for both your joy and your pain.

That's when your healing journey really begins to move forward and the outer circumstances in your life begin to change for the better. Your relationship begins to heal. More interesting and fulfilling career possibilities arise. You make new friends who support your authenticity. You begin to build spiritual community in your life.

The old you disappears along with the old story. And the new you is born.

Because you are no longer trying to run away from your pain or your sadness, you can be present for the little kid who sometimes feels terrified and overwhelmed. You know how to bring love to yourself.

Your self-concept becomes much more realistic. You know that you are not perfect and that you will make plenty of mistakes. You know that some of your lessons will be difficult. But you learn to be gentle with yourself. You cut yourself some slack. You take yourself off the cross.

When you are triggered, you learn to take responsibility for your feelings and not dump them on others. When you trespass, you ask for forgiveness. When others trespass against you, you stand up for yourself gently but firmly. You stop being a doormat. You cease being a victim or a victimizer.

This is all part of the healing process.

Real Happiness

"What does all this have to do with happiness?" you ask.

I'm glad you asked that question. This has nothing to do with the kind of happiness you see on billboards or television commercials. It has nothing to do with the overly romanticized or idealized type of happiness that is offered up to us as the goal of life. It has nothing to do with "living happily ever after."

It has to do with being present right now for the ups and downs of life in a loving, accepting, compassionate way. This is about authentic happiness. It is about being ourselves fully and being responsible for what we are creating in our life.

It is not the fake, *Madison Avenue* version of happiness decked out in diamonds and gold. It's not the Ozzie and Harriet version of happiness where people always do the right thing and no one has an anxious moment.

It is about being real as a human being, with all of the raggedness, all the pain and fear, all of the disasters of heart and mind that happen in our lives.

Sometimes life isn't pretty. It does not show up the way that we want it to. We do not always think, speak, or act in a way that we are proud of. We get angry. We get sad. We even try to shame and blame each other. But we learn to catch ourselves before we go too far astray. We learn to own our stuff and ask others to do the same. We learn to make peace, even if it happens after we have gone to war.

We learn to be present and to be real with each other. That's the kind of happiness I'm talking about. I like to call it *Real Happiness*. It means that we learn to come face to face with our fear and our pain so that we can move through them and reconnect with the joy that is our birthright.

We can cry our tears and sing our songs of gratitude and praise. When the shadows rise and the clouds gather overhead, when we hurt and don't know how to heal our pain, we do not lose our faith. We do not blame others. We do not blame ourselves. We do not blame God or the Universe. We pray for greater compassion and understanding. We submit to our lessons so that we can become stronger and wiser.

We can live a fully human life and still experience the divine presence in ourselves and in others. We know that our life has a purpose that is unfolding in each moment, even though we don't always see it.

Each day, we count our blessings. We feel fortunate to be alive and to experience the mysterious beauty of life that goes beyond up or down, black or white, sadness or joy. Each day, we learn to let go of the need to control. We learn to relax and to let life unfold in its own natural, organic way.

We trust that all will be well, and so it is. That to me is Real Happiness.

PART 2

Roadmap
for Healing

We don't do emotional healing work
to get depressed or trapped in our story.
We do it to see our reactive patterns
so that we can transcend them
and claim our freedom to choose
the kind of life we want to lead.

If Not Now, When?

There is something very profound, yet very simple I want to share with you about the nature of time.

First, I want you to understand that *yesterday is too early.*

Second, I want you to understand, that *tomorrow is too late.*

Yesterday you did not have the understanding that you have today. There is nothing that you could have done yesterday. Yesterday was simply too early. You weren't ready yet to learn the lesson or make the change.

"Okay," you say, "but I'm still not ready. I'll be ready tomorrow." And I will have to tell you. "No. I'm sorry. Tomorrow will be too late." If you wait for tomorrow to do what you are ready to do now, you may not get another chance to do it."

Do not squander the opportunities that come in this moment. They come to you because you are ready.

Don't beat yourself up because you couldn't do it before. Don't procrastinate and put it off till tomorrow.

Seize the moment. Now is the most powerful time in your life. Harness the power that is available to you now. The decision to do so will change your life!

Beginning to Put the Puzzle Pieces Together

The causes of our suffering may originate in our childhood, but we need to deal with the symptoms now and get to the bottom of them.

We need to ask, "Am I happy in this moment or not? If not, what is preventing me from being happy?"

If we think that the problem is outside of our consciousness, we are wrong. The problem is never out there. It is in here, within consciousness itself. The problem is always in our heads and our hearts.

Perhaps we have a mistaken belief or we have a paralyzing fear coming up. Okay, that is the doorway to the problem. Let's open it up, climb inside, and have a look. What do we see there?

Perhaps we see a person who is afraid of abandonment, distrusts other people and remains isolated and disconnected. S/he is afraid to leave home, except to go to church. She refuses to date because of painful experiences in the past.

We have a person who has given her power away and is waiting for someone to save her or fix her. At the same time, even when the savior knocks on her door, she isn't going to open it. She's too scared.

Now, please read this person's energy and tell me what you see. What is the nature of her energy?

It's withdrawn, passive, protected, hiding behind a wall. Correct?

Okay, so what's the answer? Some people might say, "Well, let's burn down her house and she'll have to come out."

But they don't realize that she would just find another house, another place to hide. So burning down the house doesn't work. This is not about houses or anything external. It is about consciousness.

What has to change within consciousness?

As a first step, she needs to learn to acknowledge how much fear she has. She needs to say, "Yes, I am afraid to go out. I am afraid that other people will judge me or reject me."

That's a start. But we already know this has nothing to do with "other people." It has to do only with her. The blocks to happiness are in her head and heart.

So we ask her, "Tell us about your fear. What happened to you that makes you so afraid?"

And we learn that she recently broke up with her boyfriend and this brought up a lot of feelings of abandonment that go back to her childhood when her father died. She was just four years old. And we learn that part of her is still four years old and she misses her Daddy and she thinks maybe Daddy wouldn't have died if she had been nice to her younger sister like Daddy asked her to.

We see there's the emotional pain of abandonment and there's false guilt being carried by this four-year-old girl who feels inappropriately responsible for her father's death.

We see that the four year old feels overwhelmed. And she keeps pulling on the heartstrings of the 36-year-old woman. The little girl is terrified and she wants some love and some soothing from her Mommy.

But Mommy had to be the strong one to survive Daddy's death. She had to be the breadwinner and she worked long hours. Sometimes the little girl didn't see Mommy for 2 or 3 days. And when Mommy was around, she was irritable. She wasn't very loving or patient with the little girl.

Because the little girl never had Mommy to love her or Daddy to protect her, she grew up feeling pretty insecure. And she kept desperately looking for Daddy in all of her relationships with men. Of course, that didn't work.

Because Mommy didn't model affection for her, the little girl did not know how to be affectionate with the men in her life. And they would call her "cold" and "too needy." In the end, they would realize that the little girl required way too much maintenance, and they would leave her for someone else.

This was the pattern. And the 36-year-old woman wanted to end that pattern so she stayed in her house and refused to come out. She believed that if she stayed away from life, she would be safe. No one would hurt her.

And that's where we find her.

So we ask her "Do you know there's a scared little kid inside of you that needs to be loved?

"Yeah," she tearfully admits.

"And do you know that you are the only one who can give that little girl the love that she needs? You can't depend on some man to love you or rescue you. It isn't going to happen."

"I know that," the woman says.

"Okay. So give that little girl the love that she needs. Don't go right back into a relationship or you'll just repeat the same pattern. But don't give up on relationship either. You aren't damaged goods. You just need some time to heal.

"Meanwhile, take good care of that kid. Be nice to her. Go out together and have some fun. She needs a Mommy and a friend. Maybe you could be her Mommy and her friend."

In time, the 36-year-old woman will learn to be the Mommy of the four-year-old girl. Then, she will forgive herself for being mean to her sister and stop feeling responsible for her father's death.

She will become more emotionally healed and present for herself. She will make new women friends who can offer her sisterly support and affection. Because she is stronger emotionally and has more to offer in a relationship, she will stop attracting men who will abandon her.

In short, she will heal her wounds and step into her power and purpose in life. The little girl will grow up and be comfortable in the 36-year-old woman's body.

Core Wounds/ Core Beliefs

All emotional healing begins with a simple but profound idea. *Accept your experience as it is.* Stop fighting it, denying it, or trying to change it into something else.

Once you have accepted it, inquire into its cause. Ask, "What is the cause of my fear, my sadness, my resentment, my anger, my grief, my jealousy, etc." *Uncover the core belief about yourself that fuels your unhappiness, your struggle, your despair.*

Here are some examples of core beliefs:

- "I see that underneath my anger (or sadness) is the belief that I am not good enough. I don't measure up to what others want. I disappoint others. Nothing I do is ever good enough."

- "I see that underneath my fear is the belief that I will be abandoned. Whenever I care about anyone, they leave me, so I must not be worthy of love. There must be some defect in me."

Write that core belief out. Get to the bottom of it. A core belief arises from a core wound. What is the core wound?

Here are some examples of core wounds:

- "Mommy or Daddy died/abandoned me when I was four years old."

- "My Daddy or Mommy constantly criticized me and told me I was stupid and would never amount to anything."

- "Mommy or Daddy raged at me and blamed me for their unhappiness."

- "I had to take care of Mommy or Daddy (because they were strung out on alcohol/drugs, mentally ill, physically disabled, etc.). They couldn't take care of me."

- "I was neglected, taken for granted, a lost sheep that no one knew was missing. My brother or sister got all the attention. I got the message "I don't matter.""

- "I was attacked/sexually abused (by my father, uncle, brother, priest, you fill in the blank____)."

There are many types of core wounds, but they all come down to one thing: *"I was attacked/neglected/abandoned and it hurt."* Answering these key questions will help you come up with the puzzle pieces and begin to put them together.

1. What is the *dominant emotion* that permeates your consciousness?

2. What is your *core wound?* Who hurt you and how did they hurt you?

3. What is your *core belief?* What is the message about yourself you internalized?

4. What is your *reactive behavior pattern?* How did you react to the wound/hurt: fight or flight?

5. What are your *present triggers?* How does this behavior pattern show up in your life and your relationships now?

6. What is the *chain of abuse?* How are your reactive behavior patterns impacting your children or other loved ones? How is your core wound being passed on?

7. What are the *lessons* you need to learn? What *strategies for healing* can help you transform your life?

8. How can you reverse your *reactive behavior pattern?*

You might wonder why we take the time to do this obviously difficult piece of work. Is it really necessary?

The answer is "Yes. If you want to wake up, you must understand your mental/emotional triggers and the reactive patterns of behavior that originate in your childhood. If you don't understand your core wound and your core belief about yourself, you will continue to be unconsciously driven by them. You will be like a marionette being controlled by hidden strings that jerk you around when you least expect it."

How can you take charge of your life if you don't understand how you hurt and where your pain originates?

However, once you have inquired into the root causes of your pain/unhappiness and you see the psychological structure of your suffering, you can do something about it.

That is why I ask all of my students to do this emotional healing work. It is not an end in itself. It is a step — albeit an important and necessary one — on the journey to wholeness.

Here is an example of a completed worksheet:

1. *Dominant emotion:* Sad and depressed. I see that I beat myself up constantly.

2. *Core Wound(s):* Daddy was not present. Mommy was highly critical.

3. *Core Belief:* Nothing I do is good enough. I am a failure.

4. *Reactive Pattern:* Flight, introversion, isolating, becoming inaccessible, blaming/shaming myself.

5. *How this pattern shows up in my life:* I married a woman like my mother who was highly critical of me. That exacerbated my mother wound. I couldn't stand up to my mother or my wife. I ran away. I am now divorced.

6. *Is my wound being passed on?* I love my children, but I see that, like my father, I am often an absent parent. I am absorbed in my work, which is not very fulfilling. I also see that I have become a critical parent like my mother. I expect a lot from my children. It is hard for me to love them unconditionally.

7. *Lessons/Strategies for Healing:* Learn to stand up to my mother and stop trying to win her approval. Learn to be my own mother and love myself unconditionally. Love and accept my children as they are. Stop trying to prove myself and win the approval of the women in my life. Look for positive male role models, especially older men, who will encourage me and embody the father energy I didn't have growing up. Learn to take the pressure off and be more gentle with myself. Stop working so hard and being so serious. Lighten up and take time to enjoy my life. Be childlike. Learn to trust, to play, to be spontaneous.

8. *Reversal of Reactive Pattern:* Stop running away when I am scared.

A Prescription for Happiness

As you do your worksheet, please take your time and be as thorough as you can be. If you find it helpful, do this process with a friend and/or a therapist and share your story.

You may find that it is helpful to do this exercise several times over the next year. Each time you sit down to do it, you will have new understandings and revelations about yourself.

Be sure to work on and refine section seven on *Lessons/ Strategies for Healing.* Get input from others if you feel it would be helpful. This section amounts to a prescription for happiness. It gives you concrete homework to do over the next year or two.

Each one of us comes into this life with certain lessons that we must learn. There are qualities that we need to develop in order to find greater balance in our lives.

Our reactive behavior patterns stemming from our core wound and our core belief about ourselves often push us into too much introversion or extroversion. We need to bring balance.

Introverts need to learn to reach out to others, interact and get feedback. Extroverts need to take time to connect with themselves, get in touch with their feelings, and understand what is really important to them.

This is a time for you to consciously bring balance to your experience as a human being in this lifetime. It is a time to stop reacting to life and to begin creating life the way you really want it to be.

We don't do emotional healing work to get depressed and trapped in our story. We do it to see our reactive patterns so that we can transcend them and claim our freedom to choose the kind of life we want to lead.

As you are working on your *Lessons/Strategies for Healing*, you might find it helpful to describe where you want to be in your life in a year, in five years, or in ten years. Once you know what needs to be balanced in your life, it is easier to have a vision of what wholeness looks like for you.

The following section presents in a simple way the steps in the emotional healing process. Please review this section to see where you are in your healing journey and to understand the steps that you still need to take.

Healing the Wound: A Roadmap

So how exactly do we heal our wounds? What are the steps in the process? Here is a simple roadmap.

1. *Accept the wound.* It happened to you. It is part of your life. You are not going to make it go away.

2. *Remove the Shame:* Whatever happened, you must come to see that it was not your fault. You were innocent. Stop blaming yourself. There is nothing wrong or bad about you.

3. *Acknowledge your pain and share it with others.* Stop running away from the pain or trying to hide it. Get into therapy. Get help with your addictions so that you meet the pain head-on. Share your pain with others. You are not the only one who has been hurt in this way. Find a healing community where you can give and receive support and empowerment to heal and become whole.

4. *Confront and forgive your abuser.* If there are words that you need to say and you can say them, do so. If the opportunity isn't there to look your abuser in the eye, write a letter or talk into a tape recorder. Get out all of the anger and hurt. Don't hold onto it any more. It doesn't belong to you. Scream, hit, beat a pillow, let the pain go. When you are done, burn that letter or that recording. Forgive your abuser. Keep forgiving whenever the opportunity arises. There are many layers of pain and you must bring forgiveness to each one of them.

49

5. ***Stop being a victim.*** Drop your story. Stop shaming and blaming yourself or others. Get on with your life. Let the old life go. Start creating a new life.

6. ***Create a support system,*** a spiritual family that understands where you have come from and where you are going. Make new friends. Find mentors and positive role models to emulate.

7. ***Embrace your gifts*** and begin to give them. If those gifts need refinement, take a class or two. Apprentice yourself to a master. Develop your skills and talents so that you can offer your gifts freely and confidently. Everyone has something to offer. Focus on what is joyful to you and comes naturally without great effort. Take some creative risks. Fulfill your potential. Discover your life purpose. That is what you are here for.

8. ***Help others heal.*** Give back to those who are scared and wounded as you once were. Be a facilitator and a role model. Offer people hope that healing and happiness are possible.

9. ***Empower people to make their own decisions*** and to take charge of their lives. Don't become responsible for others or try to carry them through life. Teach them to be responsible for themselves and to get on with their lives, as you did.

As a general rule, our wounds heal as we learn to accept and love ourselves unconditionally. All of the steps above contribute to that goal. As love flows to the wounded places within, they begin to heal and we begin to feel stronger and more whole. Forgiveness of self and others becomes easier and goes deeper. We let go of shame and blame and learn to be gentle with ourselves and others.

Our journey of healing is not linear—it moves backwards and forwards, up and down—nor is it always pretty. However, as we move through the dark tunnel of our pain into the light of compassion and acceptance, we see just how extraordinary the healing process is. It is truly elegant and beautiful. And it is also completely—and ingeniously—authentic.

Our story is unique and its authentic power will not be lost on others. Some people will hear our story and feel that it speaks deeply to them. They will come through the door of healing because we had the courage to share our story with them.

I have said many times that when we heal, we do not heal alone.

Your healing is a beacon of light on a dark stormy night of the soul. Many ships will find the harbor because you were there to light the way.

That is the majesty of the process. That is why it is important to have hope and courage as you go through your healing journey. You are here for a reason.

Your gifts are needed. Your life does not just belong to you. It belongs to all of us.

Taking the Time to Heal

Before we begin the journey of healing, our core belief is "I am not worthy of love." When we complete our healing journey, we know without any doubt that "I am worthy. You are worthy. Every person is worthy of love."

Yet we also know that you cannot make anyone heal. Each person has to be ready to forgive self and others.

Healing is generally a gradual process of self-transformation. Once in that process, there can be no rush to the finish line. It will take as long as it takes.

Many *New Age/New Thought* pundits forget that. They want people to snap their fingers and change their beliefs or they want them to "hurry up and forgive" so that they can finish the process quickly and neatly.

But life isn't like that. People are not like that. Forgiveness takes time. And it takes willingness. Sometimes you want to forgive, but you aren't ready. That's because there is a deeper, less verbal part of you still holding onto grievances.

If you pressure yourself to forgive, you will tie yourself up in knots. You will come up with some type of politically correct forgiveness that has no roots in the source of your pain. You will say "I know I have to forgive to get an *A* in this course, so you see "I have forgiven."

Trouble is — It won't be real. It will just be another band-aid placed on the wound to cover it up. You don't need phony forgiveness. Better to tell the truth and say, "I am not ready to forgive yet" than to lie to yourself and others.

If you lie, you will pay the price. The mask of denial will be ripped off just when you are most relying on it, and you will be exposed as a charlatan and a fraud.

Why go there? Why tempt fate? Just tell the truth right now. Say, "I really want to forgive, but this anger and resentment keep coming up, so I must not be ready."

That's authentic. That's real.

If you move through this journey with honesty, you will find the shortest and best route to healing. At times, it may not look like it's the shortest route, because it will feel like you are taking two steps backward for every step you take forward. But, trust me, if you didn't step back a little when you were moving off course, you would end up in a cul de sac with no idea of how to get back. Sometimes an extra five minutes of care saves you hours of backbreaking work.

When we are committed to the journey, we learn to trust it, even when it pushes our buttons, even when our egos are squirming and complaining.

That's how we know that our feet are firmly placed on the path. We know we aren't going to run away when the weather turns rough. We know that bailing out is no longer an option.

My core belief "I am not worthy of love" is challenged every time I show up to love myself. It is challenged when I hang in there when I want to bolt. It is challenged when I say to you "I really want your love, but I'm scared because love and loss seem to go together in my life."

My core belief of unworthiness is challenged when I face my fears or see others facing their fears. It gets challenged when I see that I can lighten up on myself and hold my judgments and my mistakes with compassion.

Changing a belief in unworthiness to a belief in self-worth is a huge piece of reprogramming. Mind, body and emotions must be rewired. Synapses must learn to fire differently.

Now, every day you can repeat the affirmation "Today I love and accept myself without conditions." That is a wonderful thing to do. But it isn't going to have much impact if you don't actually love yourself during the day. It will just be a bunch of empty words.

We aren't talking about some kind of trivial, one-dimensional healing here. We are talking about a complete re-wiring of the mental-emotional body.

And sometimes that requires taking that system off line for a while or putting it on sleep mode. You can't expect the system to be running full steam ahead if major repairs need to be made.

That's why we often get sick or get into an accident when it is time to heal. We need to take the time to heal, but we won't give it to ourselves. So the universe gives us a little help. It makes it possible for us to have a few days, weeks, or months off from work.

Healing takes time and space. Giving ourselves that time is really important. For some, the gift may be attending an inner child healing retreat. For others, it may be taking a canoe trip through the wilderness. From time to time, we all need to disengage and detach from the way that we normally live our lives in order to come back in tune with who we really are.

PART 3

Showing Up
for Your Life

*To be happy you need to be willing to show up
for your life. You cannot run away
from yourself or from others.
You can't crawl into a cave and disappear.
You can't think that other people control
your happiness. They don't.*

A Topography of Happiness

By now, you have a pretty good idea of the terrain of the journey. You know that there are ups and downs, mountains and valleys. You know that you will have good days and bad days.

This is not a "pie in the sky" scenario of healing. Most of the "pie in the sky" I've encountered doesn't get eaten on the earth plane.

We aren't looking for empty promises here. We are looking for a concrete, grounded approach to personal fulfillment.

We want you to be empowered to be you. We don't want you to try to be like someone else. We don't want you looking for the kind of happiness that is shown to us in the magazines and soap operas because that kind of happiness is phony. At best, it's only skin deep.

Genuine happiness means that you have the confidence to be yourself in this world. It means that you have healed some of your wounds and discovered some of your gifts. It means that you have something to offer to the world.

Setting Realistic Goals

To cultivate joy we must get in touch with what we really want. We can't settle for what others want for us. We must discover what we care about the most, what we are willing to show up for.

Some people know that, but many others don't. Even if they think they know what they want, they still may have trouble being committed to their goals.

The best way to cultivate our purpose in life is to start showing up for everything we have committed to. If we commit to take a college course, we need to show up at every class and do our homework. If we take a demanding new job, we better show up for work on time. If we can't do that, we will sabotage our opportunities for growth and success.

If you have trouble showing up, it probably means that you have a phony or unrealistic goal and/or that you lack discipline. Try to be clear on what your issue is.

If you have set a phony goal, it's time to get real with yourself. If you are trying to please others, understand that it won't work. Reach down a little deeper and tune into what's important for you.

If you don't know what you want to do, take the time to find out. Experiment with different things. Go back to school. Volunteer. Explore your options.

Often the goals that we set are unrealistic and overly lofty. We want to skip over all the little steps and leapfrog to the finish line. We want to run before we have learned to walk. That usually results in disaster.

Setting unrealistic goals means setting yourself up to fail. You are going to give yourself the message "I can't do it" or "Nothing I do works out." Don't do that to yourself.

This is really important. Don't teach yourself to fail.

Set modest goals that you know that you can achieve. Then, as you achieve the modest goals, you can set more ambitious ones.

For example, suppose that you want to be a doctor. Start by taking a few math and science courses to see if the work is interesting to you and if you have a natural talent for it. If the answer is "Yes," then take the next step and find a school that offers strong pre-med preparation.

Don't find the school and enroll in it first. If you do that, you might find in the very first class that you hate the work and want to drop out. That strategy will waste your time and money. And it continues to teach you to fail.

The number one rule for lofty, unrealistic goal setters is: *Don't put the cart in front of the horse.* Buy the horse first and learn to ride it.

You might think that I am being facetious here. I assure you that I am not. I know a junkyard that is filled thousands of feet high with brand new carts.

Cultivating Discipline

Now maybe your goals are authentic and realistic, but you have trouble showing up. If so, you are going to have to learn to take your commitments seriously. So please don't apply to medical school yet. Learn to chop wood and carry water.

Take any job that you know you can do and be at work every day 5 minutes early. Refuse to be bored during the day. Make yourself useful. If no one is in the store, dust the shelves and clean the windows. Put your best energy into that job. Make yourself proud.

Chances are someone will notice.

I recently met with the regional director for a large hotel

chain. He had been in the business for 35 years. His first job was washing dishes. Then he became a front desk clerk. Gradually he worked his way up to General Manager. He talked about his career with a twinkle in his eyes. He was proud of what he had achieved and well he should be.

Still, I must tell you, I know many young people who are "too proud" to take a job as a dishwasher. They want to be General Manager first. They want to skip the steps.

This is false pride. It doesn't serve anyone. It just encourages laziness and lack of motivation. It just prevents us from taking the first and most important step into our empowerment.

Now, show me a person who can't wait to clean the toilets and takes pride in leaving them spotless and I will show you the next president of Microsoft or General Motors. Sure, it might take him or her thirty years to get there, but so what?

Life is a journey. It is not an endgame.

So don't do yourself in. Don't cut off both of your arms just because you don't like the kind of work that is available to you. Move those arms. Learn to pull your own weight. Learn to exercise your motivation.

If you don't exercise your motivation and your will to show up, they will leave you quickly enough, especially if you spend most of your time smoking pot, watching television, or surfing the net.

Don't be part of the lost generation who never begin the journey. Don't give up before you learn to take the first step into your empowerment.

Don't say, "I can't hit the ball" when you haven't even once shown up to the batting cage. You may be fooling yourself, but you aren't fooling anyone else.

Don't tell me what you can't do and why you can't do it. That's just your story. And it does not empower you. It keeps you stuck in your victimhood.

No, don't tell me what you can't do. Tell me what you can do. That is where we must begin.

What you can't do is the endgame. It's the sign that you have given up. It's the admission that you are unwilling to show up.

Guess what? If you are unwilling to show up, you might as well hang up your cleats or your tennis shoes, because "Ain't nothing gonna happen in your life, baby!"

You are finished. Doesn't matter that you have not learned to take the first step. The game is over.

Suicide or Rebirth

You have to be honest with yourself and answer the question "Am I willing to show up for my life or not?"

I hate to tell you, but showing up does not mean putting up a sign in your front yard that says *Person with cart seeks horse to pull it.*

You have been here for a very long time—20, 30, 40 years, perhaps even longer—waiting for that horse to show up and s/he hasn't. If you are smart, you are going to realize that the horse isn't coming.

When that realization comes, what are you going to do? Are you going to feel sorry for yourself and pack it in? Or are you going to take responsibility for your life and start pushing that cart?

You are at the primary decision-making point in your life. This is the moment when you will choose to succeed or you will accept perceived failure.

Either way, salvation isn't going to come from outside. It can come only from within. You are the one who must save yourself. Your life is your responsibility.

If you want that cart to move, you have to push it.

You might want your parents, your friends, your spouse, or your caseworker to push it, but frankly they would be doing you a big disservice. Those who enable and abet you in refusing to take responsibility for your life simply prevent you from growing up.

Better let them off the hook. It's your choice whether or not to show up for your life.

You may think that choice is a life vs. death decision. But it isn't that at all. That is just the drama you invest in it. The real choice is simply whether or not you will walk up to the plate and swing the bat.

You will say, "I can't go up there because I'll strike out."

I know that is what you believe. And it is not a very helpful belief, because it could become a self-fulfilling prophecy.

However, that isn't even the issue. The issue is not whether you strike out or not. The issue is whether you get up there when it is your time to bat.

You see, everyone else is in the game. There's nobody else to send up there in your place. Your responsibility is simply to get up there and do the best you can.

If possible, don't hold the thought "I'm going to strike out."

If possible, think something else like "I'm going to keep my eye on the ball."

If that is not possible, and you find you have a lot of fear coming up, just try to breathe. Step out of the batter's box when you need to and then step back in. Take as much time as you need. And just do the best that you can.

Understand that this is all that is being asked from you. It doesn't matter if you strike out or hit a home run. It doesn't matter.

It simply matters that you are willing to show up. That is the discipline that is necessary. Without it, there would be no game. There would be no players or fans. The stadium would be empty.

Understanding the Drama

I know that the world that we live in is a scary world. Sometimes it seems that nothing could redeem it. There is so much insanity and heartless cruelty.

But the world has always been like that. Every generation has had insanity to deal with. Every generation of humans wonders how it could possibly contribute to a world that is so broken and bent on destruction.

And every generation finds a way to step up to the plate. If it didn't, if people really didn't step up to the challenges that face them, the world probably would self-destruct.

Tuning the world out is not an option. It will not make you feel better. It will just re-enforce your feelings of despair and powerlessness.

But stop looking outward for a moment. Stop concerning yourself with the world and look within your own mind and heart. Feel your own pain and see the potential that you have to heal and get stronger. See the gifts that lie dormant within you. Are you willing to give up on yourself? Did you come to this planet just to let your talents wither and die?"

If you are getting drunk or popping pills, remember that the cause of addiction is not the substance that is being abused. It is the pain that you are trying to avoid. Pay attention to that pain. It is your wake up call.

Wake up to your potential as a human being. Stop acting like a victim. I can tell you honestly I have never met a victim who was happy.

Drop the story. Let go of all the drama. This is not a soap opera and it is certainly not a dress rehearsal. You may not get another chance to play the part you signed up for.

Don't miss this opportunity. Start taking yourself and your life seriously.

Cultivate a Sense of Humor

At the same time, don't forget to cultivate a sense of humor. Life is as funny as it is tragic. Many of the decisions that human beings make are foolish, if not downright absurd. Murphy's law seems to prevail over human affairs. It isn't uncommon that it takes fourteen guys to install a 60-Watt light bulb. Sometimes you just have to laugh. There isn't anything else to do.

So, yes, take yourself seriously. Know that what you do does matter. You can make a difference. But at the same time, when things don't work out, when the universe slams a door in your face, learn to lighten up on yourself.

Nobody gets what he wants when he wants it the way he wants it. And there are more than a few people who need to learn this lesson before their entire existence turns to mashed potatoes. Those are the people who from time to time get hit with the sour cream.

If you step back and look, it's actually funny. Sometimes, even if you are the one who gets hit, you can still see the humor in it.

A happy life is a life that finds a balance between humor and seriousness. We learn to take ourselves seriously, but not too seriously. We learn to laugh at ourselves and at all the crazy situations and predicaments we find ourselves in.

Life lived without a sense of humor is dry and brittle. When you don't laugh, how can you express joy, lightness and exuberance? There are times when we all need to lighten up. And there are times when we need to roll up our sleeves and tackle the challenges that lie before us.

We are not limited one-dimensional beings. We can learn to be and express all of ourselves. That is part of the curriculum of life.

Cultivate a Positive Attitude

This is what I am asking you to do when I say, "Don't tell me what you *can't* do. Tell me what you *can* do."

Saying "Yes" when you mean it is the most powerful way to embrace life. When everyone says "Yes," mountains are moved and miracles happen. I have seen this occur time and time again.

However, people often put obstacles in the way of any venture. They get ego-involved, critical, and find hundreds if not thousands of reasons why they can't say, "Yes." By so doing, they not only deny miracles to others; they deny themselves the same miraculous experiences.

Of course, there are times when one has to say "No." One says "No," for example, to any attempted abuse or manipulation. One says "No" to any form of trespass. One says "No" when one is asked to disrespect or betray oneself or others.

There are times to say "No." But these times are few and far between, unless one is locked into an active cycle of violence.

Most people say "No" far more than they need to. They discount opportunities. They limit themselves. They try to control others. This results in a great deal of unhappiness.

That's why it is important to cultivate a positive attitude. Now, please realize that cultivating a positive attitude does not mean pretending to be happy or stuffing your pain. It simply means seeing the opportunities for good that surround you.

Every day, we are surrounded with opportunities to grow, to learn and to move forward in our lives. The universe has many gifts to offer us if we are open to receive them. Our job is to stay open and not to shut down our hearts or close our eyes.

We don't have to make today be like yesterday. We don't need to keep making the same choices. Let us try to see what comes into our lives with new eyes or let us at least stop seeing our lives through dark glasses.

Dark glasses serve their purpose only when the sun is too

bright. Most of the time we don't need to wear them. Yet we have difficulty taking them off.

We have developed a habitual way of looking at life with a negative bias. We need to realize that. We do not see things clearly or accurately.

If you don't believe me, try this experiment. For one day, make a list of every time you say, "Yes, I can" or "No, I can't." Draw a vertical line down the center of a piece of paper. On the left side, write down the positive, hopeful things that you think or say. On the right side, write down your negative, critical words or thoughts.

Anytime you express joy or gratitude, write it on the left side. Anytime you criticize or complain, write it on the right side.

Please be honest and don't cheat one way or the other. At the end of the day, see which column is the longest. That will give you some idea of just how negative or positive your attitude is.

The goal of this exercise is not to encourage you to see life through rose-colored glasses You are not being asked to see only the bright side of life and ignore the dark side. That would be taking the practice to the other extreme.

The goal is to see life in a more balanced way. Then you can show up for both the joy and the sadness. You can show up for the challenges of life and appreciate the gifts that come your way.

Life is inherently dualistic. Both sides of the coin are going to come up. I never met anyone who could consistently get heads or tails. Everyone gets his or her share of both.

Of course, you could be the exception to the rule, but I wouldn't bank on it!

Is the Glass Half Empty or Half Full?

Some people say, "Don't see the glass as half empty. See it as half full." Well, I have news for them. Half full is half empty!

The coin has two sides and you are not going to make one side go away. You aren't going to get rid of the lows of life any more than you are going to get rid of the highs. Everyone I know spends half of his or her time in the trenches and the other half on the ridgeline.

We all like the view at the top, but we aren't going to have it all the time.

We don't need false hope. We don't need pretense. We already know that pretending to be happy only works for the first five minutes. Your close friends and your family members know how happy or unhappy you are.

You aren't going to fool anyone, so don't bother trying to put a happy face on life. On the other hand, don't put a sad face on life either.

Life is hard enough without your adding more crap to the pile.

Remember, someone has to shovel that stuff and it might be you. So ease up.

Just take life as it comes. Don't interpret it. Don't dress it up. It isn't good or bad. It just is.

Just let it be and try to dance with it. If you get lemons, make lemonade. If you get tomatoes, make pizza.

Lao Tzu, the great Taoist mystic, gave us some really good advice. He told us to remember the mountaintop when we are in the trenches and to remember the trenches when we are on the ridgeline.

Life is constantly changing and so are we. There are plenty of ups and downs for all of us. So we better not take anything for granted.

When you are sad, be sad. Don't make yourself jump through hoops and pretend to be happy. But, at the same time, realize "this too shall pass."

And when you are happy, be happy. Don't apologize and act morose. But, at the same time remind yourself to savor the joy while it is here because it may not be here tomorrow.

Don't be attached to the highs or the lows. Neither one is going to last. Just be present with each one as it arises.

Remember you are human and so is everyone else. So be easy on yourself and try to extend that same graciousness and generosity to others. That will do more to create happiness in your life than 4 billion smiley faces.

Staying Real with Yourself

Some people tell you "Don't sweat the small stuff," and it's always nice when we can do it. But we can't always drop our fear, our anxiety, and our reactivity.

The only people I know who aren't "sweating the small stuff" are the ones who, in that particular moment, are not being triggered. But tell them "Don't sweat the small stuff," when the steam is erupting from the top of their heads and you'd better get out of the way pretty quick.

"Be happy right now" is a great idea, but what happens when you are not very happy? Are you going to reach behind your back and turn the happiness switch back on?

I don't think so. But I encourage you to try it to see if it works.

The reality of life is that sometimes the little fishes swimming toward us seem huge and overwhelming like a shark about to bite. And in those moments it is hard to pretend that "sharks are cool" or "big teeth are no big deal."

Some people have a talent for denial. It seems to work well for them and keeps the sharks away. But most people don't have that talent.

So I don't want you to feel bad if you aren't too good at denying your emotional reality. Personally, I think it's better to be in touch with your emotions than it is not to be.

On the other hand, your emotions can push you around a lot. They can even rough you up. Once you get stirred up emotionally and start reacting to life, you can totally lose your equilibrium.

So being in touch with your emotions is tricky business. It doesn't mean reacting to those emotions and rushing off to make havoc like a bull in a china shop.

The people who own the china shops don't like that very much. And who can blame them?

So if you are going to react, put the china away before you blow up and try not to put your foot through the door when your girlfriend runs away from you and hides in the bathroom.

You think I am kidding, right?

No, I am not kidding. People who are emotionally reactive hurt themselves and others. Ask any cop who has to respond to a domestic violence call.

Being with your emotions means recognizing when you are angry, or sad, or jealous. When you recognize anger, you are conscious of it and you are much less likely to be driven by it. When you acknowledge your anger verbally to yourself and others, you are less likely to put your fist through the wall.

We don't want to stuff our emotions or make a mockery of ourselves by pretending that we aren't feeling what we are. But we don't want to allow our emotions to explode either.

We want to let them come up so that we can look at them.

We want to bring our awareness to how we feel and take responsibility for that. That way we don't attack others when we get angry with them.

That goes a long way toward creating peace and happiness in our lives. It's hard to live a peaceful, happy life if you are always going to war.

The truth is that each one of us is responsible for everything that we think, feel, say and do. We can't blame others or make our experience their responsibility.

It isn't.

So we have to start getting a grip on our own consciousness and experience. We need to pay attention to our thoughts and feelings. We need to shine the light in the one place where it will make a profound difference in our lives. We need to learn to look honestly at ourselves.

To meet our Core Self we must reclaim
our innocence. That is how we find
our gift and learn to give it.

PART 4

Embracing
Your Gifts

*Every day we are surrounded with opportunities to
grow, to learn and to move forward in our lives.
The universe has many gifts to offer us
if we are open to receive them.
Our job is to stay open
and not to shut down our hearts
or close our eyes.*

Say No to Self Betrayal

When we are in pain, we begin to wake up. We realize what we don't want. We don't want to recreate the painful situations that we have created in the past.

We need to say "No" to the old patterns of self-betrayal. We need to stop giving our power away to others and begin to live our own lives.

That means that we stop living from the outside-in and begin living from the inside-out. We cease trying to live the way that others want us to live and begin to ask ourselves what we want.

Getting to know who we are and what we want is essential if we are going to be reborn as authentic people. The old persona — the mask that we wore to appease or please others — must be ripped away so that we can see what is behind it.

Behind the mask is the wound and behind the wound is the Core Self. As we acknowledge the wound and begin to heal it, more and more of our Core, True, Essential Self begins to reveal itself to us.

Very few of us know this essence. That is because very few of us heal our wounds and create the pathway to true Self knowledge.

Opening to the Core Self and the Gift

Our Core Self is not wounded. It cannot be. It exists prior to the wound and it comes into the fullness of its being, revealing itself in all its splendor, when the wound is healed.

Your Core Self is the jewel-like spark of light that you have come here to nurture, to empower, and to shine upon the world.

Your Core Self always bears a great gift that you must learn to give. At first you may not know what this gift is, so discovering the gift becomes the first step in your authentic empowerment.

Once you know what your gift—or bundle of gifts—is, you must acknowledge it, nurture it, develop it, refine it, trust it, become confident in your ability to share it, and begin to actively offer the gift to all who show up in your life to receive it.

When you are able to do that, you step into your Life Purpose. You know what you are here on the planet to do and you begin to do it. Nothing brings you greater joy or fulfillment than this.

The perfect irony, of course, is that those who can receive your gift best are those who have been wounded in the way that you were wounded. Those people belong to your House of Healing. By helping them to heal, you can complete the last stages of your own healing journey.

Your gift offers inspiration and hope to others with similar hurts and struggles. And you become a role model and a guide showing others how to awaken and access their own gifts.

There Are Many Gifts

When we think of the word "gift," we often think of some artistic or intellectual talent, but there are many types of gifts. Here are some of them.

- *Creative Gifts* (Entertaining/Uplifting others by Singing, Dancing, Painting, Writing, Playing Music, Acting, etc.)

- *Emotional Gifts* (Nurturing, Support, Healing, Listening, Encouragement, Empowerment, etc.)

- *Physical Gifts* (Athleticism, Coordination, Stamina, Physical Strength, Great Health, etc.)

- *Intellectual Gifts* (Powers of Memory, Discrimination, Logic, Analysis, Clear Thinking, etc.)

- *Psychic Gifts* (Telepathy, Empathy, Intuition, Prophecy, etc.)

- *Spiritual Gifts* (Understanding, Compassion, Acceptance, Love, Peace, Joy, Oneness, etc.)

Here are some of the many gifts that are now being offered in our spiritual community.

- The Gift of Hands-on and Energy Healing

- The Gift of Surrender

- The Gift of Forgiveness

- The Gift of Acceptance

- The Gift of Responsibility

- The Gift of Caring

- The Gift of Honest/ Non-Blaming Communication
- The Gift of Devotional Singing/Chanting
- The Gift of Writing
- The Gift of Public Speaking
- The Gift of Facilitating
- The Gift of Yoga, Tai Chi, Qi Gong, Paneurhythmy
- The Gift of Visual Expression: Painting, Sculpture, Collage, Photography
- The Gift of Listening
- The Gift of Nurturing and Supporting
- The Gift of Empowering (Teaching, Coaching and Mentoring)
- The Gift of Manifesting
- The Gift of Discernment/ Discrimination
- The Gift of Compassion
- The Gift of Cooperation/Co-Creating
- The Gift of Gratitude
- The Gift of Creating Sacred Space/Ritual
- The Gift of Connecting People/Networking

Review the list above and circle the gifts that you have. If you don't see your gift on the list, please add it to the list. Clearly, there are more gifts than the ones I have listed.

Now please ask yourself the following questions:

1. Do I accept and embrace my gift?

2. Have I taken the time to develop and refine it?

3. Am I currently trusting my gift and offering it to others?

If the answer to any of these questions is "No," please ask yourself three more questions:

1. What stands in the way of my acknowledging, accepting, and embracing my gift?

2. What stops me from developing/refining my gift?

3. What prevents me from actively sharing my gift with others?

Once you have identified the blocks to your acceptance, development and expression of your gift(s), take some time to develop concrete strategies for dissolving these blocks. Start with small strategies and take small steps. Ask yourself what you can do tomorrow, next week, or in the coming month.

Rarely do our gifts come to us fully developed and ready to share. Usually we have to go through a process of nurturing and developing the gift and then learning to trust it.

This process is essential if you are to find real happiness in your life. If your gifts are unused or forgotten, you will not harvest the joy and fulfillment that are your birthright.

The universe did its part by giving you that bright light within your heart of hearts. Your job is to find the light and learn to shine it.

Remember please, your gift is not just for you. It is for every-one. The expression of your gift not only brings joy to you; it also brings joy to others. It serves your well being, as well as the greater good of humankind. Genuine gifts can always be used to inspire and empower others.

Your gifts are the skills, talents, abilities, strengths you come into this life with. They come naturally to you and their expres-sion is both joyful and effortless.

We don't struggle with our gifts. If we do, they are not gifts, but the shackles around the gifts that come from listening to others instead of self.

Those shackles need to be removed. The treasure lies in our hearts, not in the world. Our job is to find that treasure and to bring it into manifestation in the world.

Focus on What You Want

It's important to be clear about what you don't want so that you can say "No" to the negative patterns of the past. But it is equally important to shift gears and focus on what you do want to create in your life.

Focusing on the negative patterns of thought/behavior rein-forces what is not working in your life. Focusing on the positive patterns of thought/behavior reinforces what is working.

Whatever you dwell on, whatever you give your energy and attention to, whatever you invest your emotion in, tends to grow. So consider wisely what you invest in.

Spend your time thinking about what you want to create, not thinking about what you want to avoid. Look forward to the things that you enjoy. Don't fixate on the things that you hate.

After you have embraced your pain and looked at your dysfunctional patterns, you must shift gears. You must move forward. You must leave the old, fragmented self behind and let the new, integrated self be born. Like the emerging butterfly, you must shed your old caterpillar skin and let your new multi-colored wings emerge.

To be sure, there may be growing pains. There always are. But these pains are like the pain of a woman in labor. They are intense but short-lived. When the baby is born, there is joy, and the pain of labor is forgotten.

So please don't get attached to your pain. Like old clothes you have outgrown, it really doesn't look good on you. Let the old story go and begin to create a new story.

Don't get attached to your wound. Allow it to heal. Don't be content to be a victim. Victims don't heal.

Be a Creator of your own life. Take your power back and take charge of your life. It is both your right and your responsibility to exercise your free will.

Here is an exercise that you might find helpful.

Sit down at the beginning of the week and take five or ten minutes to be silent and ask yourself these questions:

- What are my goals for this week?

- How can I nurture/develop/express my gift(s)?

- What do I want to create in my life this week?

- What actions am I willing to take to move forward toward achieving my goals?

Write the answers to these questions in your journal. Read them every day when you get up in the morning. Stay aligned with the goals you have set and the action commitments you have made.

Celebrate when you achieve any of your goals. Pat yourself on the back. Treat yourself to a hot tub or a massage. Ask a friend to join you for dinner and share your success.

If unanticipated obstacles arise, see them as challenges. Notice the adjustment that is being required and write it into your action plan for the following week.

Whatever you do, do not beat yourself up. Do not be hard on yourself. That will make it impossible for you to move forward.

Everyone has obstacles that arise in their lives. The skillful and committed person is not deterred by challenges and obstacles. They might cause him to revise his course, but they do not prevent him from arriving at his destination.

Part of what life teaches us is how to be tough and determined. You can't achieve much in life if you give up too easily. All human beings need to learn both patience and persistence. They need to learn how to hang in there when things get tough.

Having low expectations for yourself or for other people does not help. Shooting too low and shooting too high amount to the same thing. Both miss the mark.

Some people make way too little effort and others try way too hard. Neither extreme is helpful. The trick is to set realistic goals and to work diligently to achieve them. That is a surefire recipe for success.

Understanding Energy

In order to be successful in life you need to understand how energy works. Creative energy flows between two poles with opposite charges. Energy moves from the positive pole toward the negative pole, or from the male, proactive pole to the female, receptive pole.

In other words, for energy to move there needs to be a giver and a receiver, a lover and a beloved.

When energy is received, it transforms the negative pole into a positive one. In other words, the receiver becomes the giver, the beloved becomes the lover. This transformation enables the energy to continue moving, flowing back and forth between the poles or extending to another receiver.

The person who receives becomes "charged" and able to give energy back. The person who gives becomes "discharged" and therefore able to receive energy back. This results in a mutual exchange of energy back and forth between the two people.

That is why we are told, "as you give, so shall you receive."

This works until one of the two poles stops functioning. If the giver stops giving, if the receiver stops receiving, then energy cannot flow. Even if the giver gives and the receiver receives, an energetic current will not continue if the receiver does not give back.

If you understand this, you will understand why life does not just show up at your doorstep on a silver platter. If you want to receive anything back, whether it is love or money, or a job, you have to put energy out first.

Not only that. You have to put it out in a sincere, confident manner. If you put it out half-heartedly, you will get a half-hearted response at best.

There are a lot of people waiting for someone to love them and chances are they will wait a long time. If you do not give love, how can you receive it?

Now this gets a little tricky.

When you don't feel loved, when you have not received love from others, you may feel unloving and unlovable. These feelings will keep you frozen in a place of powerlessness if you don't do something about them.

Perhaps you have gone out actively seeking love and have been rebuffed or turned down. You finally get the message that love is not coming from the outside. So what can you do?

There is only one thing you can do. If energy is not coming to you from others, you must learn to give energy to yourself.

If others are not loving you, you need to begin loving yourself. This begins to transform your energy field from a negative charge to a positive charge.

The more you begin to love and be gentle with yourself, the more "charged" you get. Gradually you come back into your power and start extending love to others. Others feel your love and respond in kind.

Instead of people grimacing when you look at them, they smile back. People are happy to talk with you. They are interested in who you are. They respond to your energetic outreach.

By loving yourself generously, you fill your cup and it overflows. You begin to light up. Others notice you. They feel your energy and begin to respond to it.

Of course, this does not happen in a mechanical way. You can't love others with the expectation that they love you back. There is no real energy in that. That is called love *with* conditions. It does not work.

The only thing that works is love *without* conditions. When you love without conditions, you love and accept yourself just the way you are and you love and accept others in the same unconditional way.

That is what begins to generate energy — love without strings attached. If you don't believe me, try it. Spend one whole day loving without conditions and see what happens.

Practice Makes Perfect

Of course, it usually takes some skillfulness in this area to begin to shift your energy from being stagnant, depressed and withdrawn to being active, alert and expressive.

So don't expect results overnight.

When you first start trying to bring love to yourself in order to to effect an energetic shift, it's a lot harder than you think. At first, your critical and unloving thoughts are going to come up and you are going to realize just how much negativity about yourself you carry around.

That should not be so surprising. All of our negativity toward others has its roots in self-judgment and self-criticism.

Loving yourself without conditions means that you have to transform your relationship to yourself. You have to take all of your darkness and bring it up into the light. You have to learn to accept and bless your own experience.

We are not talking about instant salvation or enlightenment here. You are not going to transform self-hatred into self-love overnight, or even in a week or a month.

But if you begin this practice of bringing love to yourself each day, in time you will begin to feel an energetic shift. Instead of all your energy disappearing into a huge black hole in your heart, you will begin to feel energy in your heart. You will begin to feel lighter and more positive about yourself and others.

As your relationship with yourself is transformed, your relationship with other human beings and the world in general will also be transformed. You will interact with people in a more loving and accepting way and energy will come back to you from many of the people you meet.

The cycle of giving and receiving love and attention is the most important dynamic in human affairs. The well being of individuals and communities depends on it.

Love is meant to be given and received. If you try to hold onto love, you will lose it. The only way that love stays in your life is if you are constantly giving it and receiving it.

As I have said before, unhappy people tend to put the cart before the horse. They try to receive love before they have learned to give it and they are bound to be frustrated. This is not how energy works.

If you want to receive, learn to give, first to yourself, and then to others. Then the cycle of love will be established and energy will flow back to you.

Love without conditions and the love will come back to you, perhaps not from the person you offered it to, but from some person who arrives on your doorstep bearing unexpected gifts.

Remember, don't have expectations or you will get in the way of the spontaneous flow of energy. You can't direct or control the love that you give. Set it free to find its own glorious way. You won't be disappointed.

Trust, Faith, Gratitude

In the beginning of the journey, we think we can control everything. As we enter the mid-point in the journey we know without doubt that there is nothing that we control. Love and control are mutually exclusive. When you have one, you don't have the other.

We are all asked to learn to live and to love without trying to control the outcome. That means that we are asked to trust.

First, we must trust ourselves. We learn to love without strings attached and to trust that only good can come of this. We trust that what happens will be right, because our intention is right. We trust the gift we are giving.

Second, we learn to trust others to receive our love and to benefit from it in whatever way works best for them. We trust that the gift will be received as it needs to be received. We don't try to control it.

And third, we trust that the energy we are putting out will return to us in kind. We don't know how it will come or what form it will take, but we know that energy will be transformed and returned to us in the way that we need.

When it does return, we notice it and celebrate it. We inwardly feel and outwardly express our gratitude. Expressing our gratitude sends a brand new positive energy wave out into

REAL HAPPINESS

the universe. It publishes our joy and gives hope to all.

Experiencing the full cycle of *giving, receiving and giving back* strengthens our faith in the creative process. It reassures us that our needs will be met, perhaps not as we expected them to be met, but met nonetheless.

Often, when we look back at the gifts that we have received, we realize just how extraordinary and perfect they were. We can honestly say, "I'm glad this did not turn out the way I expected it to, because what happened was so much better than anything I could have imagined at the time."

The universe is brilliant in its creative inventiveness. We all participate in that creative energy, yet none of us can control it. That is a good thing, because if we could control it, we would limit its expression.

And it is so much better not to be limited and to live with gratitude and amazement in an open-ended creative process. At times, we just have to stop and shake our heads. At times, we just want to get on our knees and say to the universe, the powers that Be, "Thanks.... That was magnificent. I will remember that."

The more that we learn to trust, the more faith we have in the creative process. We know that it works with us or without us. Our choice is merely whether to try to control it or to get out of the way.

When we try to control, we are the ones who are disappointed, because life will not submit to the demands of our ego. But when we get out of the way, our energy can contribute to the creative mix and so help in the creation of something that will work for our highest good and the highest good of others.

88

At a certain point, we realize that we don't have to be in charge anymore. The universe no longer needs to do it our way.

We can take our place as one member of the orchestra and contribute the gifts that we have. We don't have to conduct or write the score.

Our job is just to learn to play our instrument well so that we can play the part that is assigned to us. When we all do that, the conductor has an easy job, and the music can speak for itself.

*Our Core Self is the jewel-like spark of light
that we have come here to nurture,
to empower, and to shine upon the world.*

PART 5

Giving Back
to Others

*Genuine happiness means you have the confidence
to be yourself in this world. It means that
you have healed some of your wounds
and discovered some of your gifts.
It means that you have something
to offer to the world.*

 ## Filling Our Cup

When we first start to heal, the needy, insecure parts of our-selves require lots of love and attention. The primary focus of our healing is receiving love and acceptance from ourselves and from others.

This is a necessary phase that we cannot skip over. This isn't selfishness. It is self-nurturing. We need to soak up the love in order to heal and gain confidence in ourselves. Then we can enter the self-empowerment phase of our journey in which we learn to stop being a victim and begin to take charge of our lives.

Before filling up our cup, we have nothing to offer others. We are too weak, too exhausted, too needy.

So first we must take time to nurture ourselves and fill our cup to the brim. That enables us to move from a negative charge to a positive charge, from empty to full. Then we are fully empow-ered and ready to serve.

Nurturing Others

When our cup is full and runs over, it is time for us give our love and attention to others who need our help. Now, just as people showed up to nurture us during our healing phase, we can show up for others and nurture them.

Still, this transition from receiver to giver is not always a smooth or easy one. We get used to having a teat to suck on that is never dry. Having a place to sleep and three meals a day is nice. We can easily become dependent on it. We don't like being asked to leave the nursery or the nest. We don't like being asked to switch gears, change roles, support ourselves and learn to support others.

But that is the nature of the healing process. As we have received, so must we give in return or our healing process will be aborted.

Those who have received and have not given back inevitably self-destruct. They lose the flow of energy in their lives and revert to their old dysfunctional patterns. If they are addicts, they return to their addiction.

People in AA know that becoming a sponsor and helping others is the key to their continued sobriety. It reinforces the choice they have made and it keeps the energy of giving and receiving flowing in their lives. It is no mystery why this program is so successful.

Guess what? If you have learned how to bring love to yourself in the depths of your pain, there are a few people the universe would love to introduce to you. Be open and receptive and it will happen. There will be a knock on your door and standing there will be someone who looks much the same as you looked two years ago.

Don't even think about shutting the door in that person's face! Your continued healing depends on his or hers. Now that you have learned to be a Mommy or Daddy to yourself, you can be Mommy or Daddy, Big Brother or Big Sister to someone else.

In other words, you are being drafted and you cannot say "No." When the call comes, you must answer it, because that is what you signed up for when you agreed to come into that body of yours. You signed up to be a bringer of love to yourself and to others.

And now your time to serve has come.

Giving Back

Just as the first phase of the healing process is all about receiving, the next phase of the healing process is all about giving. Once your head is above water and your breathing returns to normal, you need to dive back in and help someone else who is drowning.

That is not because there is some moral imperative in the universe forcing us to be "nice to others." It is because we discover, in the course of our healing process, that the greatest joy that we can experience comes when we help another person move through the same kind of pain that we have faced in our life.

Service to others binds us to our fellow human beings and to the consciousness of unconditional love more solidly than anything else. So, you see, it's not that we "have to" give back; we "want to" give back. We want to share the healing we have experienced with others.

Many of us are looking all over the globe for our life purpose when it is right under our nose. When we reach out to help someone who needs our help, our purpose is made clear. We are here to heal and to help others heal.

It's not any more esoteric or complicated than that.

Whatever your wound was, that is where you started on your

journey to wholeness. You learned to forgive yourself and others for the pain of the past. You learned to move beyond victim consciousness and to take charge of your life. *You are the living proof that healing and reconciliation are possible.*

Right now, in your town or city, others are struggling with the same core wound. They are still blaming and shaming themselves and others. Or they are in denial of their wound, trying to lose themselves in work, sex, drugs or alcohol.

You know what it means to be in denial because you have been there. You know what it means to shame and blame because you did these things too. Who else is going to reach out to these souls? Who else is capable of understanding them?

You may say "Well, that's not my responsibility." And you are right; it is not your responsibility. It is their responsibility to heal. But, as a practical matter, only a small number of them are going to heal by themselves. Most of them will not heal if you don't get their attention and say "Hey, brother or sister, come over here. Don't you see that all those others doors are closed? This door is open. Come through this door."

If it weren't for you, they wouldn't find the doorway. They would keep going through the same old doors that lead to cul de sacs. They would stay in their pain.

But you know their language. You know how they feel and the way that they think. They won't listen to others, but they will listen to you.

I'm not saying that you have to get up on a soap box or a pulpit. If you aren't afraid to share your journey of healing with others, they will find you. They will show up at your doorstep or in your class. It is absolutely miraculous how this works.

When the teacher is ready, the students show up. That's the truth. When you are ready to give back, those who need to receive your gift will find you. It's truly awesome.

It is a powerful demonstration that there is a spiritual reality at work in our lives. When we are engaged in helping others to heal, we know at long last that we are in our "right place" in this world.

Whether or not you believe in God, you cannot close your eyes to the suffering of your fellow human beings. You cannot help but feel their pain. You cannot hear their cry for help and turn away from them.

So you join the growing army of helpers that are signing up to serve all over the planet. Like you, they have moved through their pain, they have discovered their gifts and they are willing to share them with others. Like you, they are being drawn into service by the power of love. That power encourages us to share our healing with all who can benefit from it.

Healing happens very slowly when a person has to heal alone. It progresses much more quickly when a person is surrounded by people who know how to listen and can model what healing looks like.

There are many stoics who like to keep their pain to themselves. That is their choice, but it is not a choice that serves the greater good. Our pain is not meant to be held inside. It is meant to be shared with others. When it is shared, it diminishes and it becomes easier to hold that pain with compassion. That is the function of a healing community.

Many healing communities are necessary at this time. Human consciousness cannot make the evolutionary leap that is required unless we address the roots of our suffering and learn to heal our wounds together.

Until our wounds heal, peace will not be possible on planet Earth. Cooperation between countries, religions and races will be difficult if not impossible.

To awaken joy and cooperation in the peoples of Earth, communities of healing are necessary. There cannot be too many of them.

Everyone who is alive today is being asked to participate in some significant way in a community of healing. Those who heal and become empowered are asked to take leadership roles in the creation and ongoing operation of these communities.

Lao Tzu told us that if we want to heal our families we must first heal ourselves. If we want to heal our towns, we must first heal our families. If we want to heal our countries, we must first heal our town and cities. If we want to heal our world, we must first heal our countries, our races, and our religions.

Healing is a grass roots process. It moves up from the bottom, not down from the top. It is organic, not hierarchical.

This is a great blessing, because it means that what each one of us does becomes very important. If we choose to heal, healing becomes possible for our friends and family. It becomes possible for our community and our country. If we choose to heal, there is great hope for peace in our world.

Please consider that the next time your demons rise up and you think there is no hope or meaning to be found in life.

There is always hope. It just isn't going to be found out there somewhere. It is can be found only in the depths of your heart.

That is where the journey of healing begins and ends. That is where the demons are defeated and the seeds of love are sown. That is where peace in our world begins.

A Spiritual Transformation

Now I know that I said that the belief in God was not a prerequisite for this work, and it isn't. But if you have come this far on the journey, if you have learned to trust yourself and others this deeply and profoundly, then you must know that you are in the midst of a spiritual experience.

When you serve others with an open mind and a willing heart, you become like the hands and the feet of the Divine Being reaching out into the world. A higher power works through you to reach other human beings. You don't need some special training to be a servant of this power of love. You just need to be willing to heal and to help others heal.

If you look back on your life—if you remember the teachers, the mentors, the healers, the people who supported and encouraged you through your difficult times—you can see the tremendous impact they had on your life. Without them, where would you be now? They were like angels coming into your life. No matter how long the storm raged, they held your head above water.

Now you are the angel. You are the divine hands and feet in this world.

Do you see the miracle that has taken place in your life? *You have gone from being one who did not believe s/he was worthy of love to being the palpable expression of love in this world.* And that, my friend, is a spiritual transformation.

If you are not comfortable with this language, fine. You don't have to use it. But something profound has happened here. No matter what your beliefs are, you can't fail to recognize the transformation that has occurred in you and in those whose lives you have touched.

The Mechanics of Faith

Believing in God doesn't mean much if you don't believe in yourself. You have to believe in yourself and know that you are worthy of love. You have to believe in others and know that they too are worthy of love.

You have to move beyond selfish agendas into being helpful to others and see the energy that comes back to you. Then, little by little, you begin to realize that divine, unconditional love is a palpable reality. Indeed, it is the power that transforms life and enables it to realize its full potential.

Your healing makes it possible for you to step into your power and full realization as a human being. There is nothing now that blocks your way. You simply have to be yourself and walk through the doors that open to you.

At first, you may be a little wary to take the risks that you are asked to take. You may not be comfortable listening to an inner voice that tells you to walk through a certain doorway without knowing what you will face on the other side. In the beginning, you trust just a little bit and take little risks. As you realize that you are safe and guided gracefully from within, you will trust more and take bigger risks.

Your faith in yourself and your spiritual guidance are the

fruits of your willingness to trust first and then to evaluate the results. You see that your trusting leads to desirable results. In time, you begin to have faith in the process.

This isn't "blind faith." You have not closed your eyes. Indeed, you have kept them open. You have not been afraid to do a reality-test of your guidance system.

Faith in a higher power does not require that you give up reason or common sense. It simply asks you to open up to the intuitive wisdom that you have. It asks you to broaden your frame of reference and expand your consciousness.

Faith in God, or Love, or the Universal Design doesn't mean that we stop being skeptical or that we have to surrender our analytical powers. It simply means we acknowledge the presence of a transcendent energy within our consciousness and our experience. We acknowledge that there is more going on than what we perceive with our five senses.

We sense that there is an underlying purpose or meaning in life and, at times, we are able to get of glimpse of it. When that happens, we find that we are filled with love. We are uplifted. We encounter a different dimension of experience in which we feel connected to everyone and everything around us.

That is what it means to have a spiritual awakening experience. Sometimes it happens when we are close to dying. Sometimes it happens when we are experiencing the beauty of nature. Sometimes it happens when we are responding to a tragedy or disaster.

It is as if an energy comes into us, giving us strength and direction so that we can do exactly what needs to be done in the moment. We feel "inspired" or "uplifted." Our minds may be flooded with light. Our body may be on fire with the energy moving through it.

Once we have had an experience like that, it is impossible to go back to our old, humdrum way of life. We can no longer just plod unconsciously through life, because we know there is something more available. There is a transforming and transfiguring energy that is available to us if we are receptive to it and willing to connect with it.

We know in our heart of hearts that we are loved, we are wanted, we are cherished, and we are needed. What we do matters. And, if we are willing to be an instrument of love, we can be used in ways we never could have imagined.

You might think this would inflate our egos, but it does not.

It makes us ever so humble because we know that we aren't doing anything special. We are just showing up and Spirit is using us to accomplish its mission of bringing love and hope to all.

In the beginning, we feel unworthy and unprepared. We don't know what to do or what to say. We don't think we can help. Yet if we just show up and are willing to do what needs to be done in the moment, incredible things happen.

We can't take the credit for the miracles that happen, but we know that we participated in some small way in the process of their creation. We were there lending a hand or holding one. We were witnesses to something extraordinary.

Freedom and Surrender

All of our lives we are moving toward surrender. We are learning to let go. We are understanding how to be with life, without resisting it or becoming attached to it.

It isn't easy. There are times when we can't let go. There are times when we hold onto someone or something mercilessly.

When we hold on this tightly, we know that our fear is rising up. We are afraid that we will be abandoned. We are afraid that we will lose the love that we have.

Ironically, the tighter we hold on, the more certain it is that we will lose what we are so desperately clutching. Only when we unclench our fist and relax our fingers do we realize the possibility that change can occur without devastation.

The great gift that has been given all of us is the gift of free will. None of us have to be here. We have chosen to be here.

None of us have to be in a certain relationship or a certain job. We have chosen to be in that relationship or job. And we are free to choose not to be.

That extraordinary freedom that we have also makes us a bit anxious. If we can change our minds, and others can change theirs, then our life will not be stable. The apple cart will be upset from time to time.

We want guarantees that everything will remain the way it is. But life doesn't give that kind of guarantee. And, even though people give them, they don't necessarily keep their commitments.

People promise in good faith to spend their lives together and, in two years, decide that is not possible. The best employee—the one you thought would live and die with the company — decides to relocate or to take another job.

People divorce. They get sick. They die. There are no guarantees that things will stay the same.

Indeed, if you have to have a guarantee, the only guarantee you can have is the one that promises that everything sooner or later will change, shift, reinvent itself, or dissolve into nothingness.

Of course, this just drives our little kid crazy. Even if s/he wasn't insecure to begin with, the inevitability of change threatens to take him/her over the edge! After all, when abandonment is your issue, you don't want to be told that anyone, at any time, could decide to leave.

But the truth is everyone will disappear. The world will end, because you will cease to be here as its witness.

Now that idea sends the little kid into a panic attack! So we have to sit him down and tell him that everything is going to be okay and we are always going to be here for him. Other people may come and go, but he can depend on us.

We have to talk that little kid through the traumatic idea that Act Two is almost over and the drama will continue with a whole new stage set in Act Three.

Emotional flexibility is not a strong point for any wounded child. It's hard to cultivate emotional flexibility when you are in a boat bobbing up and down in the ocean in the middle of a storm! And that's where this little kid lives most of the time.

Let's face it. The little guy or girl is pretty scared and nervous. S/he wants that guarantee even though s/he's been told s/he can't have it. "Can't you just lie to me?" s/he finally asks. "Do you always have to tell me the friggin truth?"

"Yes," we tell him/her, "but I will tell it to you as gently as I can. For now, let's just take one day at a time. Let's not worry about who is going to show up tomorrow. Let's just focus on what's happening right now."

Right now we are either creating/reinforcing our attachments or we are seeing our attachments as potential causes of suffering. And if we see that potential for suffering, then we can begin to surrender our attachments here and now.

As we have said many times before, happiness cannot be conditional. It must be unconditional. No one else can make us happy. If we depend on him or her to make us happy, our happiness is conditional. And all conditions, in the end, will unravel.

So we might as well begin the unraveling now. Here's a simple exercise to do. Please write this in your journal and fill in the blanks.

"I see right now that I depend on _____ to make me happy and there will come a time when _____ does not come here anymore or _____ simply refuses to make me happy. And what will I do then?"

Slowly, deeply, breath by breath, begin to surrender your attachment to _____ and all of the other people in your life who unbeknownst to them hold your happiness hostage.

Now write: "I take responsibility for being happy as I am right now, regardless of whether _____ is here or whether _____ is being nice to me. _____ does not control my happiness and is not responsible for it. My happiness depends only on me. It is my responsibility."

If we practice surrendering into life, moment to moment,

we cultivate our freedom and set others free to make their own choices. We stop living a life that is twisted by the attempt to please others or control them.

We surrender our attachments, little by little, one by one.

When you are no longer attached to _____, you can enjoy being with him/her. You can celebrate who s/he is and be authentically present with him/her.

And that is how you create happiness: by showing up for the people who are present in your life and by accepting them as they are. This is something you do right now, right here. It does not happen in the past or future.

If you inquire into the nature of attachment, you will see that it is created in the past and reinforced in the present. To dissolve that attachment then, you simply stop reinforcing it. You drop your expectations of that person and just accept what is.

That frees you from any karmic bond or residue from the past. Now you and _____ are both free to be yourselves. You no longer need or want anything from each other.

You come into the present where the past does not exist and all things are possible.

This is the place where we want to be because this is the place of unconditional love and acceptance. This is the place of brotherhood and sisterhood. It is the place of our absolute spiritual equality.

PART 6

Joyful
Practices

If you try to hold onto love, you will lose it.
Love and control are mutually exclusive.
When you have one, you don't have the other.

Developing Witness Consciousness

Healing requires a commitment to daily spiritual practice.

One practice that can be helpful is taking 20–30 minutes each day simply getting quiet and watching your thoughts.

When you watch your thoughts, you detach from them and become the witness. You notice the thoughts that come and go in your mind, but you do not hold onto them or try to push them away. You remain neutral and just notice what is happening.

If you find yourself identifying with a particular thought or with an emotion attached to it, you simply notice that and remind yourself that you are an observer, not a participant.

In the beginning of this practice, you believe that your thoughts belong to you. But after a period of witnessing your thoughts, you begin to see them as just thoughts, not as *your* thoughts. You are no longer identifying with your thoughts. They are not you.

This is witness consciousness.

The same thing begins to happen with the emotions that are attached to these thoughts. They become just feelings, not *your* feelings. So when sadness comes up, at first it is your sadness about the fact that your mom died when you were six. But after a while it is just "sadness," or "story about sadness."

The beauty of witness consciousness is that it holds us up

above the wound so that we can look at it without identifying with it. This is very helpful.

From this place we can see how easy it is to get attached to our story. We can see how we want to make that story our identity. We want to be the wounded one who had no choice and isn't responsible for all the bad things that happened and can't work or go to school. We can see how easy it is for us to claim the role of victim and start making hundreds of excuses for why we cannot change anything in our life.

The wonderful thing here is that the witness who sees "the victim" cannot be the victim. That is the gift of awareness.

When we are aware of a pattern, we can't be in that pattern.

We can be in the pattern only if we are identified with the thoughts and emotions associated with it.

In this practice, our identification is broken and we begin to see that there is part of us that is wounded and part that is not.

And the part of us that is not wounded can bring unconditional love and acceptance to the part of us that still identifies with the wound and suffers from it.

Now within our psyche we have both the wounded child and the healer. We have the one who needs love and the one who brings it.

The components for healing are now present and the synergistic process of creating psychic wholeness can begin.

As we continue in this practice, we learn to do it throughout the day whenever we find ourselves identifying with our thoughts and emotions. The practice helps us to realize that our thoughts and emotions come and go, but we are not them.

Thoughts and emotions come into consciousness, but they

are not consciousness itself. They are simply the contents of consciousness and, as such, they keep changing, appearing and disappearing on the screen of the mind.

What does not change is the witness. The witness is always there. Sometimes s/he gets drawn into the drama of thought and feeling and believes that s/he lives there and sometimes s/he does not.

When s/he does not, there is a clarity and peace within consciousness that is remarkable. It is like a lake sparkling in the sunlight on a cloudless day. There are no shadows on the water, no gradations of light and darkness. There is just a pure reflection of light shining out in all directions.

I call this *diamond mind*. It is the pure crystalline light of consciousness communing with itself.

Such moments let us know that there is something greater than the drama of life that we can experience. There is something transcendent, yet all encompassing. We live in it and, when we notice it, it lives in us.

Gratitude and Celebration

We experience joy when we celebrate and give thanks. When we open our mouths to chant the words of love or to sing songs of celebration, we experience joy, ecstasy, bliss.

When we dance the dances of gratitude and peace, our hearts open and we feel energy moving through our hands and feet. When we bless others, when we bless ourselves, we are uplifted and so are they. When we volunteer to help someone who needs our help, we feel goodness and grace all around us.

The human spirit was meant to dance, to sing, to celebrate life. It craves this expression and cannot do without it.

That is why we go to charismatic services. We want to open ourselves to the joy that comes when we celebrate the good in all of us.

Recognizing this, one way to cultivate joy in your life is to take the time each week to gather with others to celebrate the good in life and give thanks for your blessings.

Daily and weekly rituals of gratitude and celebration help to uplift our consciousness. If you don't have rituals like this in your life, I encourage you to find them or create them.

Join a chorus, meet people from all traditions who dance the Dances of Universal Peace, spend an evening chanting, praying or drumming. Rituals like these nourish the heart.

And, in our culture, the heart is not often nourished.

There is so much in our lives that brings us down, scares us and worries us. Everytime we turn on the television or read the newspaper, we are besieged by negative news about people being raped, murdered, or killed on the battlefield.

This saddens our hearts and eats away at our hope.

You cannot keep feeding your heart poison or it will shrivel up and die. You need to feed it nourishing food. It needs to hear the good news, not just the bad.

It needs to hear about miracles, not just about disasters.

For every bad thing that happens, there is something good that happens too. We need to find the good and celebrate it.

If we don't make the attempt to do this, we will be passive victims of a media that believes that only violence and cruelty sell. It isn't true, but the media will continue to believe this until we refuse to consume the pernicious mental and emotional diet it serves up to us every day.

Are you finding the good in your life every day? Are you counting your blessings? Are you giving thanks for all of the good things in your life?

If not, why not? Just as you choose what you put in your mouth, you also choose what you feed your heart and your mind, and the hearts and minds of your children.

Don't settle for violence and cruelty. Don't be content with the bad news.

Don't go through life complaining about all the terrible things that happen in the world. Find the good things. Bring them into your heart and your home. Celebrate them with your children.

Be the one who brings hope, not the one who brings despair. Be the one who celebrates, not the one who complains. Be the one who brings love, not the one who invokes fear.

If you want to bring joy into your life, you need to change your mental and emotional diet. So turn off the TV for a day or two. Put all the electronic paraphernalia away. Turn off the cell phones, the computers, the video games. Take a break from the human obsession with motors and machines.

Celebrate the Sabbath old-style. Don't even get in your car. Take your children and spouse by the hand and take a long walk by the river, through the woods or in the park. Spend time with each other. Look into each other's eyes. Be grateful for the time you have with each other.

Life will be over in the blink of an eye. Don't miss the opportunity to express your love and your gratitude.

Giving Up Negativity

The most powerful practice we can do is also one of the most challenging. It's called "Giving up Negativity."

Make no mistake that this is an advanced practice. Don't even try it until you have done a major piece of your inner child healing work. If you do, you may be using it as a means for denying or covering up your wound.

Don't do that. Find your wound and begin to heal it. Then, when it's time to drop your story and leave the last vestiges of victimhood behind, you can embark on this challenging practice.

This practice asks you to give up complaining or being negative cold turkey. It simply says "Okay, that's enough negativity! From now on you are going to find a way to say "Yes" to yourself, to others, and to the world you live in.

If someone asks you "Do you like yellow?" and you hate it, don't say "No." Say, "I used to dislike yellow but I'm learning to appreciate it."

If someone says "Can I have some of your money?" say "Most certainly," and then give him or her whatever you feel like giving. If someone says "Four children were killed on a bus today. Isn't that terrible?" Say "Yes, and I am praying for them, for their families, for the bus driver, and for the person driving the truck that hit the bus. And I'm also praying for you and for me because this information is challenging and we need to hold it in love and not lose our hope."

No more shame and blame. It's no one's fault. We are sending our love to everyone involved.

This practice challenges you to take every event and circumstance in your life that pushes your buttons and find a way to respond to it positively.

That means that there will be times when you just have to override your doubt or your skepticism.

If your son or daughter gets a new job and it seems totally impractical and s/he has been unable to stay in a job for more than two days and s/he says "Isn't this job great?" Restrain yourself. Don't say "Here we go again." or "This is a terrible job for you." Say, "Yes, that's great and I hope this job meets your expectations."

Find a way to affirm what is happening. Find some good to celebrate in it. Find the strand of hope, however small and inconspicuous it may be, and call attention to it.

Pretend that you have just been appointed anchor of the NBC or CBS news and have been given Carte Blanche on the news that you are going to report.

Report the good news. And if you feel you have to report the bad news too, report it in a positive and hopeful way.

"Isn't this just being a Pollyanna?" you ask.

Perhaps, but Pollyanna didn't come up out of the shadows and trenches of life. She didn't face her shadow head on. She didn't look courageously at her fear and the collective fear of human beings. You did.

You did your emotional healing work. You know the cause of your pain and the pain of others. But you also know that people need hope.

People need to know that happiness is possible. People are

hungry for empowerment. And you choose to empower them.

Sure, you know that healing and empowerment are a process and don't happen overnight. But you are not going to burst anyone's bubble. You are going to tell them "Here's some great news. Here's some encouragement. May it help you commit to the journey and give you hope when hope seems hard to find."

This practice is not about denying the shadow. It is not about pretending that suffering does not exist.

That is what Pollyanna does. And that is what Buddha did before he opened the gates of the palace and went out into the streets. There he saw incredible suffering and it shook him up. He did not know that poverty, hunger and abuse existed in this world.

But once he saw these things, he could no longer be in denial. For the rest of his life, he sought a way to end the suffering of his fellow human beings.

And that is what you are committed to do also. You aren't denying the pain. You are bringing salve and dressing for the wounds. You are affirming the value of life and supporting the will to live, to learn and to transform our pain and our fear into acceptance and love.

Expecting the Positive

This is another practice that is associated with Pollyanna. Actually, it was invented by her first cousin Cinderella, who had a far more challenging life and therefore many more opportunities to practice.

As we know, things were not easy for Cinderella. She had

to clean the toilets, scrub the floors, do the laundry, chop the wood for the fire, and tote those heavy bags of ashes out into the snow. Meanwhile her sisters were living high off the hog.

They didn't have to work very hard "expecting the positive." It just rolled in off the ship.

But Cinderella was not blessed with instant ease or wealth.

She had a different sort of life. Nevertheless, she worked cheerfully and never gave up hope. Perhaps that is why hope never left her.

We all know the story. Cinderella knew that "someday her prince could come." She continued to expect the positive no matter how many insults and indignities life seemed to pile up on her plate.

Well, in the end, Cinderella's hard work and positive attitude paid off. The golden slipper eased onto her tiny little foot and it was a perfect fit. Nobody could dispute that.

Her stepmother and stepsisters could pout and be as jealous as they wanted to be. Nobody bought their story. They weren't victims. They simply got what they deserved.

The boomerang returned home. They reaped the result of their thoughts, feelings and actions. And so did Cinderella.

You can't say there is no justice in the Universe. It might take a while to play itself out, but eventually those chickens come home to roost.

Cinderella got appropriate results and so did her stepsisters.

Now what are we supposed to learn from this little story? It is after all, a moral fable. It offers us a lesson about life.

Actually this lesson is a brilliant one. Here are some of the many ingenious components:

1. Hard work won't kill you. It makes you strong. But don't forget to whistle while you work. You might as well enjoy whatever you are doing. Service counts even when you are serving a few spoiled old hags who hate your guts.

2. You have a choice: you can keep your faith or lose it. Keeping it works best.

3. In the end, you always get your heart's desire.

4. Whatever you dish out comes back to you, so watch what you are doing with the serving spoon.

5. Nobody can take away your innocence. But you can give it away by being bitter and resentful. Don't do that. Remain innocent. Hold onto your hope and gratitude. That's what the prince is looking for.

6. Sometimes you need to believe in the prince, even when you can't see him.

7. If you don't believe you deserve the prince, you will probably get a frog.

8. If a frog comes into your bedroom, take him out and put him back in the pond.

Actually, numbers 7 and 8 might be the lesson of another story. Anyway, you get my point.

Expecting the positive always works, eventually! The problem with those who do "Cinderella light" is that they give up too easily. They expect immediate results.

As soon as they are asked to do the laundry or take out the trash, they say, "That's enough. I'm out of here!"

They just aren't patient enough with the process. You can "expect the positive," but that does not mean it is going to come when you want it or how you want it.

You need to hang in there.

In my book *The Laws of Love,* the Fourth Law, the Law of Manifestation, clearly states that we manifest in physical reality only that which we care about the most and are most committed to.

So if you are not committed enough to the prince to wait for him, chances are he isn't going to show up in your life.

You have to do your part just as Cinderella did hers. If you are more like Cinderella's sisters—spoiled, impatient, and too proud to take out the trash—you can "expect the prince," but it isn't going to work.

Princes aren't that stupid. Give them a little credit please.

They know the difference between a hard working princess and a spoiled bitch!

Of course, princesses aren't stupid either. They know which frogs are just frogs and which are really princes in disguise. They don't just pucker up for any old frog.

So there you have it.

The question is not "Does the practice of *expecting the positive* bring results?" The question is "How diligently are you willing to practice?"

Luck isn't totally random or gratuitous. It is the result of hard work and a positive attitude on our part and the unexpected, serendipitous reply of the universe.

Rising Above the Drama

Shakespeare told us: "All the world's a stage, and all the men and women merely players."

Life is 95 percent drama, and 5 percent essence. That means that we live primarily in the drama. We take things very seriously and spend the majority of our time reacting unconsciously to the events and circumstances of our lives.

If we could step off the stage for a moment and watch the drama unfolding, we would realize how absurd it is. We would see that we make life much harder and more complicated than it needs to be.

When we rise above the drama, we can see what the essence is and attend to it. We can let the rest just slide off our shoulders. We learn to focus on what is really important and not to sweat the small stuff. Then, even the sharks turn into minnows.

Each one of us must find a way to get off the stage and see what's happening there from a more transcendent perspective. Otherwise, we become mired in the muck of life and it's hard to find clarity or peace.

There are many ways to do this. For some people, meditation works. We take time every day to detach from the drama and to find the place within that is centered, peaceful, and connected to our essence.

Taking a long walk every day can serve the same purpose. When we walk up in the mountains, by a stream or on a deserted beach, far away from human sights and sounds, we recharge physically, emotionally, mentally, and spiritually.

Personally, I find it is impossible to be depressed, agitated or self-obsessed when I am surrounded by towering trees, rushing water, wind or surf. The sounds of nature calm my body, cleanse my mind, uplift my emotions, and awaken my spirit.

My life is healthiest when each day I seek out some remote place, in the woods or on a beach where I can breathe deeply and let go of the demands and pressures of my life. As I walk, I remember who I really am. I reconnect to my Core Self. And then I can return to my human life more centered and clear about what is really important.

Balancing mental work with daily physical exercise is also important. When the needs of both mind and body are met, clear thinking results. The mind can focus on solving the practical problems of life and no longer dwells on its own fears, anxieties and neurotic obsessions.

Each of us must find some kind of daily ritual that helps us move our energy out of our head and into the rest of our body. Otherwise, we become imbalanced and begin to get stressed out.

Most of the drama that we experience happens not out there in the world, but in our own minds. We begin thinking about something and before we know it, our minds are off to the races. We start remembering things that happened in the past, and often emotions like fear, guilt, or resentment come up.

We try to function at work or home as if nothing is happening internally, but it doesn't often work. If we don't take time to be with our feelings, we are easily triggered by others and they in turn are triggered by us. The result is more drama, more shame and blame, more hurt feelings. We say a lot of things that we don't really mean. We attack or withdraw. We push each other away.

Finding a daily ritual that helps us get centered and process our feelings is an essential aspect of caring for ourselves and treating others with respect. When we can take responsibility for our own emotional experience, instead of dumping our feelings on others, we avoid unnecessary drama and it is easier for us to communicate with each other honestly and compassionately.

So now get out that notebook and make a list of some of the ways that you can rise above the drama. Ask yourself these questions:

- What rituals help me to slow things down, let go of the small stuff, and see what's really important?

- What rituals help me lower my stress levels, balance the needs of mind and body, and allow me time to process my feelings when they come up?

- What rituals can I do every day to rise above the stage and see the play of life with greater detachment and perspective?

- What rituals help me connect to the Spirit within and get centered in my Core Self?"

When your list is complete, choose one daily ritual that you can incorporate into your life for the next week. Then watch to see the difference it makes in the quality of your life. You can add rituals or revise them as necessary until you find the right combination for you.

How do you know it's working? You know it's working when your life stops being deadly serious and you learn to lighten up and have a little fun. You know it's working when you get our of your head and into your heart, when you stop being so stressed out and on edge, when you have time to breathe, to exercise, to be present in a relaxed way for yourself and others.

Keeping It Simple

Wherever you are in your healing journey, please do not be overwhelmed by the work that lies ahead. We need to take this slowly. We need to put one foot in front of the other.

We aren't going to heal if we put too much pressure on ourselves or think that we are running out of time.

Let's take the pressure off and realize that we have plenty of time. We heal as we are ready to heal and not a day sooner. We can't rush the process. It will take as long as it needs to.

Our job is merely to show up and to do what we can today.

Remember the word KISS. It stands for "Keep it simple, stupid." Of course, you aren't stupid, unless you set huge, unrealistic goals that you can't possibly achieve.

Don't do that. Stay grounded. Keep it simple. Get used to setting realistic goals and to achieving them. That way you will be able to build on your success.

Remember "the journey of a thousand miles begins with a single step." So take the first step now. Don't worry about the second or the third one.

By doing this, you are teaching yourself how to succeed.

That is important, because in the past you may have done just the opposite.

Try to stay out of your head, where you are conquering worlds and building empires. Come into your heart and just put one foot in front of the other.

When you go up into your head and start getting over-whelmed or anxious, take a deep breath and ask, "What can I do now?" And don't ask yourself to do anything more than that.

Tell yourself, "This is what I can do now and so this is what I am going to focus on. I am not going to worry about all the things that I can't do now. I will just trust that somehow all these things will be addressed in their own good time."

If you know The Serenity Prayer, use if frequently. If you don't know it, learn it and start to use it in your life.

Tell yourself, "It's okay that I don't know how this is all going to turn out because I do know one thing and that's the most important thing. I know that I am doing the best that I can right now in this moment."

And then give yourself a break! Ease up and be gentle on yourself. Take another deep breath and keep breathing until you begin to relax and let go of the pressure.

Dissolving Pressure from Others

Most pressure comes from inside, not from outside. But occasionally pressure seems to come from others who have certain expectations of you that you cannot meet.

When that is the case, you have to honor yourself and speak up. Go to the person who has those expectations and say, "I'm sorry. I am trying very hard to do this, but I just can't. I can't do it the way you want it or in the timeframe that you have established."

Most people will appreciate your honesty and take you off the hook. And those that won't might need to get two weeks notice.

You are a human being, after all. You aren't perfect. The best that you can do is the best there is. End of story.

You can't get blood out of a stone.

There are times when everyone needs to ease up and take a deep breath. Sometimes we set impossible expectations not just for ourselves, but for our partners, for our children, or for our employees.

You don't want to become a slave driver because when you drive yourself in that way you get sick or have a heart attack. When you drive others that way, you lose their loyalty and affection. You end up divorced, disowned by your children, abandoned by your employees.

Pressure doesn't work, whether it comes from the outside or the inside. So find out where the pressure is coming from and deal with it. Slow things down. Ease up on yourself and others.

It's time to pause, evaluate what's happening. It may be time to revise the goal, change the strategy or the timetable. It might be time to shift gears.

When a truck comes to a steep hill and it begins to lose speed, it needs to shift to a lower gear or it won't have the power to climb the hill.

Sometimes people are like trucks. They also need to find a lower gear to negotiate the challenging terrain that lies ahead.

The ones who do not shift are the ones who burn out or fall apart. Don't be one of those folks.

Don't put too much pressure on yourself. Don't let others put too much pressure on you. Don't put too much pressure on others.

Live one day at a time. Put one foot in front of the other. Take a step back when you need to.

Do the best that you can do. More than that is not necessary, healthy, or wise.

PART 7

Radical
Acceptance

The treasure lies in our hearts, not in the world.
Our job is to find that treasure and to bring it
into manifestation in the world.

Taking Time Alone

Human beings are social creatures, but all of us need at least an hour each day to be alone. The real meaning of alone is "all one." To spend time alone is to experience our wholeness. It is to know that we are enough, that we are acceptable, that we are complete just the way we are.

This is best done by sitting or walking in silence. By not speaking or engaging with others, we can begin to experience ourselves from the inside out.

Now, just in case you wondered, you can't do this practice very well with the television or the radio on. You want to avoid most external stimulation. You want to be able to breathe and be. You want to allow the focus of your attention to shift from the mind to the heart or the belly.

Rhythmic breathing can help you to get centered in this way. So whether you sit or you walk, let your breathing be easy and steady. Find a simple rhythm that you can sustain without effort. As you breathe in this way, you will sink into deeper and deeper states of consciousness.

In these states, you are profoundly relaxed. Stress and anxiety dissolve. You move from a state of thinking or doing to a state of breathing and being. You get out of your head and into your heart. You enter into communion with yourself in a deeper way than you experience in any other activity.

Your mind is awake, but it is not focused on anything else. It is just the witness or the observer.

If you are sitting, your body is relaxed and all of the cells are recharging just as they do when you sleep. Yet, at the same time, you are present and alert.

If you are walking, your body is moving in a slow, natural rhythm. You are physically relaxed and mentally alert.

Rituals like yoga, Tai Chi, and various forms of meditation can help you to experience this kind of deep relaxation, calm and inner peace. However, you don't need a formal practice.

Just begin spending half an hour or an hour in silent self-communion every day. Focus on your breathing and use it to help you relax and sink into a deeper level of consciousness. Let this be a time when you appreciate and affirm yourself, breath by breath, step by step.

Meeting Your Needs for Belonging

Just as it is essential to spend time alone to nurture and commune with yourself, it is also essential to experience connection with others. For some people, especially for those who are married or choose to live together, some form of daily communion is necessary.

Couples who see each other every day should build into their lives at least fifteen minutes of sharing and listening in silence to each other. Another helpful practice is to hold hands with eyes open or closed for fifteen minutes. These practices are easily combined.

Other helpful practices are massaging each other, walking together in nature, and taking the time to make love in a relaxed, sensual manner that is fulfilling for both people.

Good relationships require time, attention and loving care. Daily and weekly rituals that promote this kind of care and attention are necessary to help partners stay connected in an intimate, trusting way.

Even those people who are celibate and/or not living with another person require some kind of regular contact (at least weekly) with a loving community of like-minded human beings. We all need to exchange ideas, share our life stories, give and receive hugs, encouragement and other forms of love and support.

To attempt to live in isolation from others is not a good idea for most people. For most people, it results in loneliness and depression and for some it leads to mental-emotional rigidity and various forms of self-obsession.

It is possible to live a life in which you do not spend enough time alone or in which you spend too much time alone. If there is an extreme either way in your life, you need to find ways to create more balance.

This may seem obvious to you. But I know many people who live at one extreme or the other. Many parents of young children, for example, do not have sufficient quality time alone, with each other, or with their children. This creates a great deal of stress for all concerned.

I also know of many young people and seniors who do not have friends and have not taken the time to build community in their lives. They are isolated, lonely and depressed. Their needs for affiliation and belonging are simply not being met.

It is not possible to create happiness when we have not established the basic building blocks by having quality time alone and with others. If we are not willing to do this, how will it happen?

Our happiness, as we have said, is our responsibility, not someone else's. If we want to be happy, we may have some homework to do.

Accepting Yourself

Self-acceptance is much harder than we think. We are all very hard on ourselves. Some of us are downright merciless!

Self-acceptance requires that we dissolve some of our negative habit patterns. For example, we have to clean up our "self talk." That means that we need to be aware of the times when we are finding fault with ourselves.

Whenever we notice that we are saying things to ourselves like "I'll never do that right;" or "There I go screwing up again." or "I'm such a fearful, untalented, clumsy, _____ (you fill in the blank) person"—we need to be aware of our negative self-talk and learn to be a little more gentle and compassionate with ourselves.

We need to be the witness and see these thoughts without identifying with them. "There I go beating up on myself again," we learn to say. "That's an old habit I am learning to break. It's good that I see the pattern and don't buy into it anymore."

We also need to stop expecting ourselves to be perfect, because being a perfectionist is the best way to crucify ourselves. We need to accept our human frailty, admit our mistakes and try to learn from them.

We learn to say "I can accept myself just as I am here and now, warts and all." We learn to look at ourselves in the mirror without wincing.

We know that we can always improve ourselves and become more confident, more skillful, more flexible, and more sensitive to others. We know that we are "a work in progress," but we also give ourselves credit for what we have already learned and how far we have come.

We learn to celebrate our successes and get over our failures. We learn to stop complaining and to start counting our blessings.

Each one of us is cultivating a relationship with ourselves moment to moment. How do we want that relationship to be? Do we want it to be a compassionate one or a merciless one? Do we want to bless or condemn, accept or criticize ourselves?

We need to make a clear and firm decision about that because we cannot and will not be happy if we insist on having a cruel, insensitive relationship with ourselves. Our happiness requires us to have a loving, compassionate relationship with ourselves, moment to moment.

Of course, we all lose it from time to time. We don't love or accept ourselves under all circumstances and conditions. But we learn to notice when we are starting to beat ourselves up and we bring a gentle correction. We learn to forgive ourselves in the moment.

I give all of my students the Mantra "Am I loving myself right now?" This is the most important question that we can ask ourselves. If the answer is "Yes," we can be fairly sure that we are happy and joyful in that moment. And, if the answer is "No," we understand the cause of our distress and the correction that can be made to reclaim our joy and happiness.

Accepting Others

Other people are no more perfect than we are. They are sometimes selfish. They occasionally make mistakes. They are sometimes insensitive or unskillful. There are times when they get stressed out or angry and say and do things that are hurtful.

Just as we can't expect ourselves to be perfect, we can't expect others to be either. We have to learn to be gentle and patient with others. We have to learn to forgive them in the moment.

When we notice that we are being critical or judgmental of others, we can be sure that we are also beating up on ourselves. So we need to bring awareness not just to the outward judgment, but also to the inner wound. We need to see our judgment and the wound behind it and hold them gently.

Not finding fault with others requires practice. We have to keep bringing our awareness to our judgments and keep remembering that our goal is *to accept, not to find fault.*

Initially, we may be rather alarmed by the number of judgments we are making toward others. But, in time, we learn that all of these judgments stem from our own unworthiness. By holding our judgments gently in awareness, we bring love to the wounded parts of ourselves.

The more that we engage in this practice, the less impact our judgments have within consciousness. We can notice our judgments without making them real or justifying them.

Feeling guilty for judging—or judging our judgments—only intensifies the negativity within consciousness. We must remember to bring acceptance, not judgment, to our judgments.

I know this probably seems like mumble-jumble to you right now, but when you begin working with this practice you will see what I mean.

The awareness "I am judging" held compassionately within consciousness has a totally different impact than the judgment itself when we buy into it or make it real.

We need to remember what the nature of this work is. We are not asked to "stop judging." That would put way too much pressure on us and make this practice difficult, if not impossible.

We know that we are going to judge and that is okay. Our work begins after the judgment comes up. Our work is to see that judgment—so it is not habitual or unconscious—and hold it gently.

Bringing awareness automatically brings the possibility of correction, acceptance and love. On the other hand, unchallenged judgments, habitual patterns of blaming or shaming, fuel our deep-seated fear, guilt and unworthiness.

Much of our work of accepting others involves working with our own consciousness and bringing love to ourselves. When we bring love to the one who is judging, judgments fall away.

Nevertheless, we also have to be aware of our trespasses against others. We need to recognize when our words or actions are hurtful to other people.

When we notice that we have acted in an unkind or cruel way toward someone, it is important that we "own it," acknowledge that we have made a mistake, ask for forgiveness and, if possible, make amends. We also need to resolve to learn from our trespass and not repeat it. This takes great courage and commitment.

In addition, let us recognize that one of the great challenges in interpersonal relationships is accepting the differences between people. Accepting the dignity and worthiness of our adversaries or opponents is essential if we are going to find real happiness in our lives. Most of the people we meet in life are going to have values, ideas, cultural/religious beliefs and experiences that are very different from our own.

It is easy to accept others when they accept us and agree with us. It is much harder to accept them when they don't like us and disagree with our ideas and values.

However, we can't make our love and acceptance of others conditional on their having the same upbringing or experience that we have. We have to allow for differences and accept them tolerantly, if not graciously.

When we accept differences, they do not have the power to divide us. When we don't accept them, they can create constant strife and discontent.

Our goal here must be to treat others as equals and to respect their experience or point of view, even when it differs from our own. Peace between people does not depend on their agreement so much as it depends on their mutual acceptance and respect.

So we learn to give other people a break. We let them have their experience and we drop our judgments about it. We ease up on others. We stop condemning. We stop finding fault. We work to accept the people in our life just as they are.

Accepting What Is

One of the hardest things for us to admit is that life is okay the way it is. We don't need to edit it or change it.

Even if we thought we could improve the hand that life has dealt us, we would have to admit that we haven't been given the option. The master dealer didn't come and ask us for our opinion.

We didn't choose to sign up for breast cancer or an automobile accident. We didn't choose to lose a loved one, to be sexually abused by our uncle, or to see our business go belly up.

These things just happened and we have to deal with them. We have no choice but to accept what has happened in our lives. If we have been wounded by these events, we must learn to tend to the wound so that we can heal it.

Some of us feel disappointed in life because it did not or does not meet our expectations. We may even be bitter about this. We may blame others. We may blame God.

But bitterness and resentment don't improve our situation and they don't help us to heal. So if we want to be happy, we have to give them up.

We have to stop complaining and learn to move on with our lives. We must find a way to take our power back and exercise our free will. We need to stop making excuses and give up being a victim, because victims don't know how to be happy.

Every event that occurs in your life offers you an opportunity to accept or reject, to appreciate or complain, to cooperate or resist. The tactics of denial/resistance do not create happiness. Indeed, they impede it and simply waste time and energy.

No matter how many rounds you make on the merry-go-round, you will keep coming back to the same choice. Are you going to work with what is happening in your life, or are you going to refuse to work with it? Are you going to say Yes or No to your life?

The answer that you give to these questions will make it pretty clear what your happiness quotient is. Those who say "No" to what is happening in their lives are squandering their opportunities to grow in wisdom and strength. They are refusing to learn the skills that are necessary to succeed in life.

Sometimes life is hard. That isn't just true for you. It is true for all of us. Does that mean you are going to refuse to show up? Do you really think you even have that option?

I like to think of life as a flavorful sauce and we are all meatballs cooking in the sauce. Sometimes the heat gets turned up on the stove and we have to deal with it. If we get out of the sauce too soon, we will be uncooked meatballs. Sooner or later, the universe will notice that and throw us back in the pan.

The bottom line is that we can't get out of the sauce until we are completely cooked. Anything else would be premature and against the laws of cooking.

To put this another way, sometimes we just need to accept the challenge of life, suck it up, and learn the lesson in front of us. Everyone who is here has important lessons to learn. You and I are no exceptions.

Of course, I am aware that sometimes life comes right up to you, looks you in the eye, smiles at you, and smacks you over the head with a 2 x 4. When that happens, there is absolutely nothing you can do about it. There is no way you could have been prepared for it.

Maybe it happened because you were getting a little too cocky. Maybe it was just because you were in the wrong place at the right time.

No matter. You have to accept it, because it happened.

Forget trying to understand why! If there is a why you are going to know what it is without thinking about it very much. And if there isn't, it doesn't matter how hard you think about it or how many times you take it apart and put it back together again. You aren't going to figure it out.

Sometimes you don't like what happens, but you just have to lump it. Your goose gets cooked. There's nothing you can do about it.

It isn't the first time and it probably won't be the last. Complaining about it isn't going to help.

God doesn't hate your guts. The universe isn't out to get you. You simply got a wake up call. That means that you have no choice but to wake up!

So get out of bed and put the coffee on. You might as well go to work a little earlier this morning. Evidently, there is something you need to do, even if you don't know what it is yet.

Just show up and it will become clear. We don't get awakened so rudely if there is nothing here for us to do.

Accept the lesson. Say, "Okay, God, you got my attention, so bring it on. I'm ready to listen. I'm ready to learn."

And if you don't believe in God, talk to the guy who swung the 2 x 4. He can tell you what the message is. And, frankly, it doesn't matter if you hear it from the one who sent the message or from the messenger!

Once you get the message, you can make the adjustment life

is asking you to make. And then, maybe it all begins to make a little sense.

In retrospect, you can see why you needed to slow down or shift gears. You can see that you were going to hell in a hand basket and somebody had to grab the handle and yank it.

You can't take it personally. And it's good that you didn't.

Now you can be an alert and happy player, because from now on it isn't very likely that you are going to zone out or nod off to sleep.

You learned your lesson well. You don't need another 2 x 4 across the temples.

After a while, you begin to see that the people who get hit the most are the ones who aren't paying sufficient attention.

Some are taking things for granted. Others are just being careless or smug.

When you look around now, you can almost see it coming.

So you might say to your coworker or your buddy, "You might want to know that there is a guy with a 2 x 4 who is following you around."

They might look at you like you're crazy, but at least you know that you gave them a head's up. It's really amazing how many people get tipped off and don't pay any attention.

Answering the Call

Life is permeated with mystery and often its meaning is elusive. But the message that comes when you are betraying yourself or others is usually a pretty obvious one. That's a good thing because most of us aren't very smart. And even the smart ones often hear only what they want to hear.

The message is usually something like "Wake up. Stop giving your power away. Stop hurting others. Stop betraying yourself!" The message usually comes with "shock and awe," as well as a rather pungent dose of pain. That's so we won't ignore it.

The other part of the message you will hear if you keep listening is, "There is something for you to do in this life. There is a gift that you have that is needed. There is something for you to contribute. Don't ignore the gift or refuse to give it."

You are asked by the universe to stop being a victim and to become a creator of your life. You are asked to develop a relationship of trust with yourself and with the world in which you live. Whether you believe in God or not, the message is all about your purpose and the spiritual meaning of your life.

So you have to keep listening. From now on you are going to be having a "conversation with God" or at least a dialog with the guy who is holding the 2 x 4. Better get used to it.

You are being plucked out of the hoard of victims and complainers and being drafted into an army of helpers and healers who want to make a difference in their lives and the lives of others. You are getting your assignment for this embodiment.

Now maybe you don't believe in all this. That's okay. Just play along. You don't need to believe in the purpose of your life to be willing to fulfill it. If you are willing to show up, if you are willing to help out, you will be put to work. There's plenty to do.

There are many souls who are unhappy, depressed, suicidal —you name it. Maybe you remember a time not so long ago when you were there.

So you know how forlorn and abused one can feel being a human being. You are no stranger to fear, pain and shame.

That is why you can be so useful now.

You know how to go into the trenches. You know the words to say. You know what people need to hear. You know the message that delivered you from despair. Does it surprise you that you are now the one who must deliver it?

The universe has an intelligent design, even though it often seems to be well disguised. There is some kind of method in its madness.

We have to laugh at the times when the madness seems to dominate. It isn't our fault. It isn't even the fault of the head Curmudgeon.

Murphy works at all levels of existence. He even has a relative who was canonized!

Things get nebulous and confused not only here on Earth, but even in the higher realms, where wisdom and grace purport to dominate. That is why a sense of humor is necessary.

Even the Divine Being, from time to time, has to laugh! And sometimes when S/He does, it seems that the belly of the heavens seems to shake from side to side.

We too must take time to laugh at the utter absurdity of life. When we do that, we get a little relief from the heavy burdens we carry around. Indeed, for a brief moment, we get a glimpse of what it might be like to be free of our fear, our pain, and our shame.

For a moment, we begin to imagine being free from the vice-like grip of our human egoic experience. We start to float off with the angels to a lighter, happier, and more gentle place.

But then—perhaps because we are afraid to let go totally—our thought system grounds us again. And we pick up our heavy suitcases and move forward to climb to the crest of the next hill.

That, my friends, is what Sisyphus did. He labored hard, pushing that huge boulder to the top of the mountain, only to find the weight of the stone unbearable and to feel it slip out of his grip and tumble back down the mountain.

Fortunately for him, the boulder did not flatten him or send him careening down the hill. He lived for another day and another attempt to push that boulder skyward.

What most people don't know about Sisyphus is that on his umpteenth try, Sisyphus had an awakening experience. Just as the boulder began to tumble back down the hill, Sisyphus was overwhelmed with the absurdity of it all and began to laugh uncontrollably. Indeed, he laughed so hard that even God became jealous.

From that day onward, Sisyphus just hung out on the mountain, watching the wildflowers come and go. He knew that to every thing there was a season, a time to live, a time to die, a time to push heavy stones around, and a time to let them go.

To make the story short, the time for letting go had come in Sisyphus' life. There will come a time like that for all of us.

Until then, let us not forget to laugh. The quality of our lives very much depends on our cultivating a cosmic sense of humor.

If you don't believe me, just ask that guy with the 2 x 4!

Thanks to him, sadness and sorrow have no chance. Thanks to him, you and I are leaving the past behind and awakening to the happiness that is our birthright.

I bow to the bright being within you. May joy light up your heart and dance in your eyes. May it spread like a wildfire. May it uplift the hearts and sparkle in the eyes of all the beings who share your life!

Paul Ferrini is the author of over 30 books on love, healing and forgiveness. His unique blend of spirituality and psychology goes beyond self-help and recovery into the heart of healing. His conferences, retreats, and *Affinity Group Process* have helped thousands of people deepen their practice of forgiveness and open their hearts to the divine presence in themselves and others.

For more information on Paul's work, visit the web-site at *www.paulferrini.com,* email: info@heartwayspress.com or write to **Heartways Press, 9 Phillips Steet, Greenfield, MA 01301.**

Explore the Other Spiritual Mastery Books

If you like this book, you may want to read the other books in the series. They are briefly described below.

The first book — *The Laws of Love* — contains ten essential spiritual principles that we need to master in order to heal and step into our life purpose.

The second book — *The Power of Love* — contains ten spiritual practices that help us connect with our Core Self, our Source, and the gift that we are here to give.

The third book — *The Presence of Love* — helps us understand the masculine/feminine aspects of the Divine and shows us how to embody the unconditional love that will heal us and our planet.

The fourth book — *Love is My Gospel* — looks at the life and teachings of one spiritual master (Jesus) as an example of what is possible for us.

The fifth book — *Real Happiness* — shows us how to heal our wounds at depth and awaken the joy that is our birthright.

The sixth book — *Embracing Our True Self* — describes the three stages in the process of healing and transformation and offers case histories of people who have transformed their lives in our community.

Paul Ferrini's *Course in Spiritual Mastery*

Part Six: Embracing Our True Self

A New Paradigm Approach to Healing Our Wounds, Finding Our Gifts, and Fulfilling Our Spiritual Purpose 192 pages $13.95
ISBN # 978-1-879159-69-3

Part Five: Real Happiness

A Roadmap for Healing Our Pain and Awakening the Joy That Is Our Birthright
160 pages $12.95
ISBN # 978-1-879159-68-6

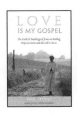

Part Four: Love is My Gospel

The Radical Teachings of Jesus on Healing, Empowerment and the Call to Serve
128 pages $12.95
ISBN # 1-879159-67-8

Part Three: The Presence of Love
God's Answer to Humanity's Call for Help
160 pages $12.95
ISBN # 1-879159-62-7

Part Two: The Power of Love
10 Spiritual Practices that Can Transform Your Life
168 pages $12.95
ISBN # 1-879159-61-9

Part One: The Laws of Love
A Guide to Living in Harmony
with Universal Spiritual Truth
144 pages $12.95
ISBN # 1-879159-60-0

Paul's In-depth Presentation of the Laws of Love on 9 CDs

THE LAWS OF LOVE
Part One (5 CDs) ISBN # 1-879159-58-9 $49.00
Part Two (4 CDs) ISBN # 1-879159-59-7 $39.00

Audio Workshops on CD

Seeds of Transformation:
Set includes: Healing Without Fixing, The Wound and the Gift, Opening to the Divine Love Energy, The Laws of Love, The Path to Mastery.
5 CDs   ISBN 1-879159-63-5 $48.00

Two Talks on Spiritual Mastery by Paul Ferrini
We are the Bringers of Love   CD 1
Surrendering to What Is   CD 2
2 CDs   ISBN 1-879159-65-1 $24.00

Love is That Certainty
ISBN 1-879159-52-X $16.95

Atonement:
The Awakening of Planet Earth and its Inhabitants
ISBN 1-879159-53-8 $16.95

From Darkness to Light:
The Soul's Journey of Redemption
ISBN 1-879159-54-6 $16.95

Relationship Books

Dancing with the Beloved:
Opening our Hearts to the Lessons of Love
ISBN 1-879159-47-3
160 pages paperback $12.95

Living in the Heart:
The Affinity Process and the Path of Unconditional
Love and Acceptance
128 pages   paperback   ISBN 1-879159-36-8
$10.95

Creating a Spiritual Relationship
128 pages   paperback
ISBN 1-879159-39-2 $10.95

The Twelve Steps of Forgiveness
120 pages   paperback   ISBN 1-879159-10-4
$10.95

The Ecstatic Moment:
A Practical Manual for Opening Your Heart
and Staying in It
128 pages   paperback   ISBN 1-879159-18-X
$10.95

Christ Mind Books

Part 1   Part 2   Part 3   Part 4

Love Without Conditions ISBN 1-879159-15-5 $12.00
The Silence of the Heart ISBN 1-879159-16-3 $14.95
Miracle of Love ISBN 1-879159-23-6 $12.95
Return to the Garden   ISBN 1-879159-35-x $12.95

The Living Christ ISBN 1-879159-49-X paperback $14.95
I am the Door hardcover ISBN 1-879159-41-4 $21.95
The Way of Peace hardcover ISBN 1-879159-42-2 $19.95
Reflections of the Christ Mind hardcover $19.95

Wisdom Books and Audio

Everyday Wisdom
A Spiritual Book of Days
224 pages paperback $13.95
ISBN 1-879159-51-1

Wisdom Cards:
Spiritual Guidance for Every Day of our Lives
ISBN 1-879159-50-3 $10.95
Each full color card features a beautiful
painting evoking an archetypal theme

Forbidden Fruit:
Unraveling the Mysteries of Sin, Guilt
and Atonement
ISBN 1-879159-48-1
160 pages paperback $12.95

Enlightenment for Everyone
with an Introduction by Iyanla Vanzant
ISBN 1-879159-45-7
160 pages hardcover $16.00

The Great Way of All Beings:
Renderings of Lao Tzu
ISBN 1-879159-46-5
320 pages hardcover $23.00

Grace Unfolding:
The Art of Living A Surrendered Life
96 pages   paperback   ISBN 1-879159-37-6 $9.95

Illuminations on the Road to Nowhere
160 pages   paperback
ISBN 1-879159-44-9 $12.95

Audio Books

The Economy of Love Readings from *Silence of the Heart, The Ecstatic Moment, Grace Unfolding* and other books.
ISBN 1-879159-56-2 $16.95

Relationship as a Spiritual Path Readings from *Creating a Spiritual Relationship, Dancing with the Beloved, Miracle of Love* and other books. ISBN 1-879159-55-4 $16.95

The Hands of God Readings from *Illuminations, Enlightenment for Everyone, Forbidden Fruit, The Great Way of All Beings* and other books.   ISBN 1-879159-57-0 $16.95

Love Without Conditions Read by the author, 3 CDs.
3.25 hours ISBN 1-879159-64-3 $36.00
Also available on cassette tape for $19.95

Order any of these products on our website:
www.paulferrini.com

or call toll free in the US: 1-888-HARTWAY

The website has many excerpts from
Paul Ferrini's books, as well as information
on his workshops and retreats.

Be sure to request Paul's free email newsletter,
his inspirational weekly wisdom message,
and a free catalog of his books
and audio products.

Heartways Press
9 Phillips Street
Greenfield, MA 01301
413-774-9474   Fax: 413-774-9475
www.heartwayspress.com
email: info@heartwayspress.com..

Heartways Press Order Form

Name_____

Address_____

City _____State _____Zip _____

Phone/Fax_____ Email*_____

Please include your email to receive Paul's newsletter and weekly wisdom message.

Title ordered	quantity	price

TOTAL _____

First Class Shipping: one book $4.95, two books $5.95   _____

3 books (shipped UPS ground) $6.95   _____

Additional books, (UPS ground) please add $1 per book   _____

TOTAL _____

For shipping outside the USA, or if you require rush shipping,
please contact us for shipping costs phone:

Send Order To: Heartways Press 9 Phillips Street,
Greenfield, MA 01301   413-774-9474
Toll free: 1-888-HARTWAY (Orders only)
www.Paul Ferrini.com   email: info@heartwayspress.com

Please allow 1–2 weeks for delivery. Payment must be made by check or credit card (MC/VISA/AmEx) before books are shipped. Please make out your check or money order (U.S. funds only) to Heartways Press.